HOPE IS NOT LOST

Staying Connected with God
in the Midst of Depression

DERRIN DRAKE

WestBow
PRESS
A DIVISION OF THOMAS NELSON

WestBow Press books may be ordered through booksellers or by contacting:

WestBow Press
A Division of Thomas Nelson
1663 Liberty Drive
Bloomington, IN 47403
www.westbowpress.com
1-(866) 928-1240

Because of the dynamic nature of the Internet, any web addresses or links contained in this book may have changed since publication and may no longer be valid. The views expressed in this work are solely those of the author and do not necessarily reflect the views of the publisher, and the publisher hereby disclaims any responsibility for them.

Any people depicted in stock imagery provided by Thinkstock are models, and such images are being used for illustrative purposes only.

Certain stock imagery © Thinkstock.

ISBN: 978-1-4497-5345-0 (sc)
ISBN: 978-1-4497-5346-7 (hc)
ISBN: 978-1-4497-5344-3 (e)

Library of Congress Control Number: 2012909054

Printed in the United States of America

WestBow Press rev. date: 05/25/2012

TABLE OF CONTENTS

PREFACE

THERE SEEMS TO BE A void between the church and the mental health system in explaining causes for depression and treating it. The main problem is that the church has a tendency to over-spiritualize causes and treatment for depression and the mental health system has a tendency to underutilize spiritual care in treatment. A person's spiritual care is then left in the hands of the mental health system which is not equipped to address it or a church system which could blame the person, pushing them further away from God. And although there are Christian agencies that cater to religious and spiritual care for patients suffering from depression, they are limited in their capacity to provide biblical causes and treatments. Essentially, biblical explanations are rarely, if ever, used. It is safe to say that many people neither have a sound biblical view of God as the source of their healing and recovery nor find hope from the Word of God in their treatment process.

Over my twelve years in the mental health field, this void is exactly what I have experienced when working with patients suffering from depression. During my time as a case manager, at an outpatient case management agency, I remember getting the mental health code's rules surrounding spiritual care placed on my chair by some unknown person. These rules were not placed on anyone else's chair as I had found out by asking around. I believe the placement on my chair was a response to my documenting a patient contact where I pointed out a patient's hypocrisy of using illegal drugs but yet trying to witness Jesus Christ to others. The mental health code is a set of rules governing people treating patients with mental illnesses. During my five years at a Christian inpatient psychiatric facility, I have also witnessed interesting dilemmas arise with the spiritual care provided to a patient. These dilemmas are likely due to restrictions of the mental health code which provide the rules to abide by when facilitating spiritual care. Essentially, we have secular mental health codes that are not biblical or spiritual directing spiritual care. There is much good that happens with spiritual care at the inpatient facility where I work, but I witness the lack of meeting those spiritual needs as well. The church I attended and the ministries in which I have been involved have also had their limitations in addressing those that happen to be suffering from depression. I have been a firsthand witness of people being blamed for their suffering or told that the cause was some *hidden sin, unconfessed sin,* or *demon.* In light of these multiple problems, this book is written in hopes to provide those suffering from depression, as well as those treating someone with depression, guidance and hope from the Bible.

Note: Bible verses are taken from the New American Standard Bible (NASB) unless otherwise noted.

INTRODUCTION

PERSONAL EXPERIENCE WITH DEPRESSION

"I DON'T LOVE YOU, AND I don't think I ever did" were the words that began an eerily familiar journey back down a road of depression. It had been several years since my initial bout with depression, following a breakup with a longtime girlfriend, but the enemy had returned.

The initial bout was an arduous one that stole several months from my life and was followed by several years of residual effects. The darkness of night was my friend, as it would lend itself to sleep, but there also seemed to be an unwanted darkness during the daytime hours that lent itself to a resident heaviness combined with complexities of thoughts, behaviors, and emotions.

Eventually, I became depressed to the point that I barely got out of bed for about seven months. This withdrawal and isolation to my bed was combined with lack of appetite, low motivation, low energy, and irritability at the least of things. My thoughts were consumed with negative themes of worthlessness and the inability to be loved. Questions of *why* were rampant in my mind, and I had ruminative thoughts about wanting the relationship with my girlfriend to be mended. During my college courses, I neglected assignments and ended up doing poorly those few semesters. These intense symptoms lasted for several months. Then I was finally able to start participating in life again, but with effort on my part. For several years, the symptoms, although lessened, still lingered.

My second bout of depression was also the result of a situation I had no control over. My wife had decided to leave me and spoke those devastating words mentioned above. During this bout, I lost thirty pounds within a few months, was tired all the time, had poor energy, had a poor appetite, was easily irritated, withdrew from friends and family, had a negative outlook on life, and was quite anxious. This lasted only about four months and then these intrusive symptoms improved. The difference between these two situations was that in the second episode, I was seeking God.

The wisdom and understanding I gained from these two episodes were that unfortunately there will be valleys in life, but Jesus is "the Alpha and the Omega"[1] and will be there at the beginning and through until the end. Jesus is also Immanuel, meaning "God with us," [2] so He is also there through the entire journey of the valley.

CHAPTER ONE

DEPRESSION IS A PERVASIVE PROBLEM in our society and the most common mental health disorder leading to disability in America.[1] There could be as many as twenty million people in the United States who are impacted by depression.[2] This pervasive disorder strikes people across all socioeconomic lines, so no one is exempt from its impact. Insurance companies that pay for a depressed person's treatment are acutely aware of the direct and indirect costs of depression, and they want the most effective treatments available in order to curb the costs.[3] "The direct economic costs include those associated with recognizing, caring, treating, preventing and rehabilitating depressed patients in primary and secondary health care and social care. The indirect economic costs result from depressed individuals being unable to maintain their usual economic role, and include the effects of illness on work attendance and productivity, the costs of long-term disability and premature mortality, and the loss of productivity of family members involved in a caring role."[4] The annual economic burden of depression is about forty four billion.[5]

SIGNS/SYMPTOMS OF DEPRESSION

The word depression is often used casually and its meaning can be quite vague. A person could easily say "I am depressed" and really not be depressed at all. The person could simply be experiencing the normal ups and downs that all humans experience as part of life. Therefore, it is important to have a good understanding of depression in order to accurately diagnose it. A person should always lean on professionals to accurately diagnose a depressive disorder to avoid misdiagnoses.

In the medical field, the *Diagnostic and Statistical Manual of Mental Disorders* (DSM) is used by professionals in diagnosing many different psychiatric disorders. This manual is published by the American Psychiatric Association and is in its fourth edition.[6]

Persons suffering from depression experience a variety of symptoms, and each person might not suffer the same symptoms. However, the primary signs and symptoms are

- persistent sad, anxious, or "empty" feelings;
- feelings of hopelessness or pessimism;
- feelings of guilt, worthlessness, or helplessness;
- irritability, restlessness;
- loss of interest in activities or hobbies once pleasurable, including sex
- fatigue and decreased energy;
- difficulty concentrating, remembering details, and making decisions;
- insomnia, early morning wakefulness, or excessive sleeping;
- overeating or appetite loss;
- thoughts of suicide, suicide attempts; and
- aches or pains, headaches, cramps, or digestive problems that do not ease, even with treatment.[7]

MEDICATIONS

Medications are the primary weapon in combating depression and other mental health disorders. The psychotropic antidepressants used to treat depression are Prozac®, Paxil®, Zoloft®, Celexa®, Effexor®, Cymbalta®, Lexapro®, Wellbutrin®, Remeron®, Desyrel®, and Pristiq®. Medications can be a wonderful tool in stabilizing a person's symptoms of depression. This was demonstrated with medications being the primary agent in deinstitutionalization in America. Deinstitutionalization was a process, in the 1960s, in which mentally ill people were let out of institutions with the development of medications. Of course there was also a political and economic agenda behind it as well, but it was medication stabilization that specifically led to discharge from mental institutions and allowed patients to function outside the hospital setting.[8] In regard to other medical conditions, medications are essential in keeping someone alive (e.g., bacterial infections, diabetes, heart conditions, etc.). There have been wonderful advances in the medical field in regard to medication's effectiveness in treating illnesses. It is also important to note that medications are inherently good and created for the good of mankind.

Sometimes medications are necessary for treating depression, but not always. Medications can be helpful but are not hundred percent effective in taking away all of a person's symptoms of depression. Typically, multiple medications are used for treatment of depression, and a person might need to be switched from one antidepressant to another.

1. On Abilify.com, it states that Abilify can be an "add-on" medication when an antidepressant is "not enough." Further, the website states, "Some people being treated for depression may continue to experience depressive symptoms. Depression is a common and treatable illness, but it may take a few tries to find an antidepressant that works for you."[9]

2. On Seroquelxr.com, the message is this: "If you have unresolved symptoms of depression, you may need more than one medication to help manage your condition. If you've taken an antidepressant for 6 weeks or more and still have symptoms of depression, talk to your doctor. He or she may decide to adjust your treatment plan and consider adding a medication like SEROQUEL XR to help you treat your depression."[10]

In his article "Depression: More Than a Chemical Imbalance," Carey Krause, DO, says, "Unfortunately, depression continues to be a difficult illness to treat. Few people respond immediately to medication, and some require a trial of a second or a third medication before they experience relief."[11] Many individuals still have symptoms of depression even on large doses of medication or a combination of medications. Therefore, we must have an accurate picture of medications and their ability to remove all symptoms of depression.

This is the information given regarding medications on the website Mental Health America: "Medicine can ease depression symptoms. But the first medicine you take may not be the right one for you. If you still have symptoms after initial antidepressant treatment, you should not give up. It may take some time for the medicine to start working, or it might help to change the amount you take. Or you may need to try several different medicines, take more than one medicine, or add other forms of treatment, such as psychotherapy. Keep in mind that finding the right medicine(s), or combination of treatments for TRD [Treatment Resistant Depression], can take some time"[12]

There are some individuals who are not helped by medications, have severe complications or side effects to medications prescribed, have had an increase in suicidal thoughts, and have formed medical disorders such as diabetes. More medications almost always lead to the possibility of more side effects and the increased risk of medication interaction.

Doctors and scientists have done their best to cure or eradicate depression with medications, but depression remains prevalent in our society. Medications may restore a person's functioning, help them cope, or stabilize a person in order to function in their daily activities, but there is no cure for depression or mental illness. Medications only impact chemical levels of what is already present in the brain(serotonin, norepinephrine, or dopamine) but do not heal a person. Depression is, therefore, considered a lifelong illness.

CULTURE AND MEDICATIONS

The idea of treating everything with a medication is a serious error that has infiltrated our society. People tend to want to feel nothing, and patients have told me that they want to "feel numb" or "nothing at all." If there is any symptom of depression present, they want medication in order to remove it. In my experience, some people were taking medications as a way to mask their need for resolving grief, loss, or situational issues in their life. In one specific case, I counseled a woman who used as much medication as she could in order to deal with sadness created by her father's death several years before. She suppressed her feelings, which only resulted in an uncomfortable increase in her depression and anxiety. Instead of grieving and resolving these issues, she simply altered her emotions and mental state with medications and continued to live in misery. She was simply medicating the grieving process.

Finally, we need to mention the placebo effect. A placebo effect is the effectiveness of a treatment or medication based on a person's belief that the treatment or medication will work prior to it starting. Placebo treatment is "not the absence of treatment, just absence of active medication." In a National Institute of Mental Health article titled "Placebo, Antidepressants May Lift Depression via Common Mechanism," the results of active medications and placebos are explored in their impact on brain activity. They assert that "whether it's a widely prescribed medication or a placebo, a successful treatment for depression must trigger common pattern of brain activity changes." In their random study, they chose seventeen middle-aged men who had been hospitalized for depression and gave them active medication or a placebo. The results: four men receiving actual medications improved, four men receiving a placebo improved, and nine men showed no improvement at all. Both groups of men showing improvement had brain activity changes. An interesting finding was that those with the placebo showed much faster brain activity changes.[13]

CURRENT THEORIES FOR THE CAUSE OF DEPRESSION

The current theory is that there are multiple causes for depression. Most likely, depression is caused by a combination of genetic, biological, environmental, and psychological factors.[14] And there are shortcomings with each of these theories. An example of contradiction arises in the genetics explanation for the cause of depression. Although there are patterns within families that allow the medical field to say that there is a genetic component, there remains difficulty in explaining why, in some cases, one member of a family has depression and no one else does in the family line. In reality, anyone can be impacted by depression regardless of family history, upbringing, socioeconomic status, or ethnic background. Despite all the research information available, there is still much difficulty in pointing out a specific cause for depression and the research into specific causes and most effective treatments is ongoing. Reviewing all the research information one could rightly conclude, although there is much known about depression, much is needed to be learned. It is necessary to point out that psychology and psychiatry are not perfect sciences and should not be touted as such.

OTHER POSSIBLE CAUSES

Vitamin B$_6$, Folate, and B$_{12}$

"There is a prevailing hypothesis that insufficient concentrations of B vitamins are associated with depression."[15] Further, Vitamin B$_6$, Folate, and Vitamin B$_{12}$ are essential in the metabolism of essential amino acids that "are critical to the production of neurotransmitters and methylation in the brain."[16] And we know the levels of the neurotransmitters dopamine, serotonin, and norephinephrine are associated with depression. In fact, antidepressants target these neurotransmitters in the brain. Research between the connection of the low B Vitamins and depression is ongoing.

DEHYDRATION

Dehydration can have negative impact on the brain and the body, as "the brain tissue is about 85 percent water and the body is about 70 percent water."[17] In terms of chronic dehydration, "depression is a common symptom."[18] Dehydration affects levels of serotonin as a result of the amino acid tryptophan not being converted into serotonin in the brain. Dehydration can also "deplete other essential amino acids in the body. Studies have shown that an incessant shortage of amino acids can contribute to feelings of dejection and inadequacy, as well as feelings of anxiety and irritability."[19] The Bible talks about "anxiety in the man's heart"[20] causing depression concurring with the scientific theory of a link between anxiety and depression. Being hydrated could be helpful in some cases of depression, and there does appear to be a link between dehydration and depression. [21]

OMEGA-3

The American Journal of Psychiatry indicates that there is a possible link between deficiencies in omega-3 fatty acids and mood disorders. The article states that "deficits in omega-3 fatty acids have been identified as a contributing factor to mood disorders and offer a potential rational treatment approach." Further, "biological marker studies indicate deficits in omega-3 fatty acids in people with depressive disorders, while several treatment studies indicate therapeutic benefits from omega-3 supplementation," particularly the fatty acids found in fish. However, ongoing testing and studies need to occur in order to test the "efficacy of omega-3 supplementation for unipolar and bipolar depressive disorders."[22]

VITAMIN D DEFICIENCY

A number of studies report some connection between vitamin D levels and the risk of depression. "Low vitamin D levels may be related to depression rather than contributing to the disorder. In addition, an increased risk of depression may be related to several vitamin D—sensitive diseases." It is surmised that "given the evidence, it is possible that vitamin D could have a positive effect on those who suffer from depression."[23]

OBESITY

One interesting note to make is there could be a possible link between obesity and depression. But it is difficult to say if depression impacts obesity or vice versa. "One study, published in *Pediatrics*, found that the longer a child is overweight, the more he or she is at risk for depression and other mental health disorders."[24]

MEDICAL CONDITIONS

Other possible causes for depression are also linked to medical conditions. These conditions could be hypothyroidism and chronic pain. "Although hypothyroidism and depression are distinct diseases, they are interconnected in many people's lives. Sometimes depression is the first indication that a person's thyroid is underactive (hypothyroid). Depression is more significant in people with hypothyroidism than those without thyroid problems. To help doctors determine whether depression is actually caused by or associated with hypothyroidism, depressed patients need to be screened for thyroid disorders."[25]

Identifying the medical condition as the direct cause of depression is proving to be quite difficult, which could be a result of depression coexisting with other medical conditions. There is ongoing scrutiny around certain medical conditions, such as a pain condition known as fibromyalgia. There is an argument as to whether or not fibromyalgia is a legitimate medical condition instead of a psychosomatic condition. In short, psychosomatic conditions originate in the mind itself, but display themselves in the physical body.

FORMS OF TREATMENT FOR DEPRESSION

In addition to medications, there are many kinds of psychotherapies. Psychotherapy is a way to help people with a mental disorder, understand their illness, to learn new ways to manage stress, to address unhealthy thoughts, and to address unhealthy behaviors so they can function better in their lives.[26] Psychotherapy can be a the sole treatment a person receives, depending on the severity of their symptoms, or they can combine therapy with medications.[27] The most common forms of treatment for depression are a combination of medication and therapy.[28] Therapy is important as "quality psychotherapy can help a depression sufferer begin to feel better within the first sessions."[29] Cognitive Behavior Therapy (CBT) and Interpersonal therapy (IPT) are two of those therapies, but in my experience, CBT is more widely used than IPT. The National Institute of Mental Health, in their review of the Sequenced Treatment Alternatives to Relieve Depression Study, states that "switching to or adding cognitive therapy (CT) after a first unsuccessful attempt at treating depression with an antidepressant medication is generally as effective as switching to or adding another medication, but remission may take longer to achieve."[30]

COGNITIVE BEHAVIOR THERAPY (CBT)

CBT is blend of cognitive therapy and behavioral therapy and was developed by Aaron T. Beck in the 1960's.[31] This therapy has been widely used by mental health providers over the past several decades and shown to be helpful to "patients with depression, panic disorder, phobias, anxiety, anger, stress-related disorders, relationship problems, drug and alcohol abuse, eating disorders, and most of the other difficulties that bring people to therapy."[32] A person's thoughts are normally the central focus, as they are what influence a person's mood. These thoughts are "automatic thoughts" or the thoughts that pop into a person's head following an event. For example, a man asks a woman out on a date and she says no. His automatic thought could be *she must think I am not attractive.* These automatic thoughts could not be true and need to be addressed per influence on mood. These automatic thoughts are influenced by our assumptions about ourselves and our "core beliefs." Core beliefs are "absolutistic statements about ourselves, others, or the world."[33] These "core beliefs" are developed throughout childhood and based in a person's experiences.[34] The process of CBT is "learning to change maladaptive assumptions and core beliefs" to decrease "negative, distorted automatic thoughts" and develop "new assumptions and core beliefs."[35] With these changes comes less distressing situations for the individual in terms of anxiety and depression.

INTERPERSONAL THERAPY (IPT)

Interpersonal therapy (IPT) is used to treat depression and dysthymia, which is a less severe form of depression.[36] The current manual-based form of IPT used today, was developed in the 1980's by Gerald Klerman, M.D., and Myrna Weissman, M.D. IPT is based on the idea that improving communication, interactions, and how a person relates to other people to treat their depression.[37] IPT helps identify problematic behaviors and helps guide a person in the change of that behavior. This is often where the therapist will help the patient learn to express themselves in appropriate ways. IPT also "explores major issues that may add to a person's depression, such as grief, or times of upheaval or transition."[38] Sometimes IPT is used along with antidepressant medications. Relationships from the person's past might also be examined as a way to be function better in current relationships. Studies vary on how effective IPT really is and could be influenced by the patient and severity of their disorder."[39]

Electroconvulsive Therapy (ECT)

Electroconvulsive Therapy (ECT) is one of the several brain stimulation therapies available. ECT is a treatment for people who "cannot take antidepressant medications,"[40] whose antidepressant medications are not effective in treating symptoms, or whose depression is considered "life-threatening." A person is under anesthesia during the treatment. ECT is a course of "six to 12 treatments, administered at a rate of three times per week, on either an inpatient or outpatient basis." During the treatment, "electrodes are placed at precise locations on the head to deliver electrical impulses. The stimulation causes a brief (about 30 seconds) generalized seizure within the brain, which is necessary for therapeutic efficacy.[41] The person receiving ECT does not consciously experience the electrical stimulus . . . The most common side effects of ECT are confusion and memory loss for events surrounding the period of ECT treatment. The confusion and disorientation experienced upon awakening after ECT typically clear within an hour and then the "patient is usually alert and can resume normal activity."[42] Unfortunately, the majority of people will have to continue to take antidepressant medications in conjunction with the ECT treatments to maintain any benefits from them. [43]

Repetitive Transcranial Magnetic Stimulation (rTMS)

Repetitive transcranial magnetic stimulation (rTMS) is another brain stimulation therapy available for depression and is less a less intrusive treatment than ECT. In 2008 the FDA approved TMS for the treatment of major depression. Unlike ECT, rTMS uses a magnet instead of an electrical current to activate the brain.[44] This treatment is indicated when a person has not responded to "at least one antidepressant medication,"[45] suffers from treatment resistant depression, or cannot handle medication side effects of those prescribed medications.[46] Stimulation targets the specific areas in the brain believed to be "involved for mood regulation."[47]

Vagus Nerve Stimulation (VNS)

"In 2005, the U.S. Food and Drug Administration (FDA) approved VNS for use in treating major depression in certain circumstances—if the illness has lasted two years or more, if it is severe or recurrent, and if the depression has not eased after trying at least four other treatments."[48] Despite FDA approval, VNS remains a controversial treatment for depression because results of studies testing its effectiveness in treating major depression have been mixed.[49] This treatment is primarily utilized in the treatment of epilepsy. The procedure uses a small device that sends a mild electric impulse to the brain via the vagus nerve.[50] VNS likely impacts the brain in some way which impacts neurotransmitter chemical levels."[51]

Other brain stimulation therapies include Magnetic seizure therapy (MST),[52] and Deep brain stimulation (DBS).[53] "Brain stimulation therapies hold promise for treating certain mental disorders that do not respond to more conventional treatments" and research is ongoing for treatment efficacy, reduction of their side effects, safety, and effects on the brain.[54] But they are more intrusive treatments when compared to psychotropic medications and the psychotherapies available.

Treatment from Spiritual Care

Among mental health workers, there are many varying beliefs of Christianity and the Bible, making it difficult to provide concrete and definitive treatment in this area. Many social workers may not hold any Christian beliefs at all and could possibly lead people astray from a belief and a reliance on God. Spirituality from a biblical standpoint is important in a person's recovery, but there remain significant shortcomings in the field of social work today.

Those patients who are involved in non-Christian and mainstream agencies, such as community mental health, psychiatric institutions, case management and outpatient counseling, have limited access to and support from the spiritual side of their treatment. This is in spite of many mental health recipients viewing their spiritual life as the most essential part of their makeup. Therefore, the spiritual aspect is often under-addressed or not integrated into their treatment at all. Recipients of this type of care are indoctrinated with scientific explanation. Therefore, they rely on methods outside a biblical context for explanation and treatment.

Most agencies believe that medications and therapy alone are the frontline weapons in treating depression. The need for a combination of medications and counseling shows that depression cannot be solely explained and treated by medications, as a person may also have maladaptive thoughts and behavior patterns. Those who look at depression from a purely scientific perspective may say that counseling may simply just reroute pathways in the brain. I would like to add that the Bible can do this exact same thing when we apply it to the pathways in the brain. And the Bible is the only book that has stated, through God, that "all Scripture is inspired by God and profitable for teaching, for reproof, for correction, for training in righteousness; so that the man of God may be adequate, equipped for every good work."[55] The meaning of "inspired by God" literally means "God-breathed." Unfortunately, most mental health agencies put the body and the soul (mind, will, and emotions) first and very little importance on the spiritual.

CHAPTER TWO

CHRISTIANS AND DEPRESSION

T HE IMPACT OF DEPRESSION HAS not escaped Christians. Yes Christians can experience depression, as they are not immune from its reaches! Depression can cause significant problems for Christians in terms of how they explain the causes and treat it. Some Christians have a view that it is all a spiritual leaning toward a demonic influence, a lack of a person's faith, or a person's sin. Others may adhere to spiritual explanations, such as depression as a test from God, a punishment from God, a thorn of the flesh, or a person's cross to bear. There are traps in these explanations, and they have the tendency to point at the person as the cause of their depression. We can summarize that sometimes these aforementioned reasons explain the cause of the person's depression, but not always.

What cannot be debated is that depression can be extremely disruptive and debilitating for some people suffering from the disorder. Carey Krause expounds that depression robs individuals of the willpower to take care of the simplest tasks and that their waking moments are an experience of ongoing misery where nothing brings them pleasure and leaves them with a deep sense of hopelessness.[1]

DEPRESSION'S IMPACT ON A PERSON'S SPIRITUAL LIFE

We can surmise then that depression is experienced by a Christian in the same way as others who are left without the ability to experience pleasure and with a sense of hopelessness. This inability to experience pleasure is important when it comes to being in a mutual relationship with God. Christians might experience the inability to be loved by others and by God and believe that God has forsaken them. They might also neglect spiritual disciplines important in their walk with God.

Another complicated area for those who are depressed is that of suicidal thoughts. Suicidal thoughts can come in different types; sometimes they are passive where individuals are more wishing they were dead or hoping God would take them in their sleep, and other times they are active and come with intense urges. These thoughts can be fleeting or occur on a daily basis where the person might think about suicide most of the day.

Two examples of the results of depression on spiritual life are taken from two patients with whom I worked at an inpatient psychiatric facility. One patient, a female and in her fifties, had not experienced any problems with depression until her husband died after many years together. From the time of her husband's death, she began to experience a spirit of heaviness and a sense of hopelessness. When she experienced these feelings, she would have thoughts in her mind that God had abandoned her and was somehow displeased with her. She then went one step further in thinking that she must be feeling this way, not because her husband had died, but because she had somehow committed some sin (what she called "participating with the devil"). Along with this thought, she started to have suicidal thoughts. She thought that if she participated with the devil, she was now completely rejected by God. The hopelessness stemming from her thoughts about God's rejection eventually led her to take her own life, following discharge from the hospital.

The second example is a gentleman who was hospitalized because of very similar symptoms, in that he was very depressed and hopeless. In talking with this man, he divulged that he was hopeless because he had rejected God when he was young and now God was rejecting him. It would almost become an argument with this man when discussing anything about God's forgiveness and God's love for him. These ingrained thoughts about God led him to believe that his situation was hopeless. The end result was that he wished he were dead. He could not bear living with the hopelessness that came from believing God had rejected him. This man was living a miserable existence, as he could not connect with God per his depression and hopelessness. This man left the hospital only mildly improved, as a major burden for him was living day to day believing God had forsaken him.

Lying or Deceiving Spirits

I have encountered many people with depression before, but these two aforementioned cases were somewhat different in that I believe these two had a lying spirit. The Bible talks about a lying spirit in 1 Kings 22:22-23 (KJV). A lying spirit goes forth into a false prophet's mouths and speaks a lie which the people believe; they are then destroyed in battle. They believed the lie to their own destruction. Likewise, these two had a lying spirit attached to their minds and needed to be "renewed in the spirit"[2]of their mind. Essentially, anything that is against the Bible is a lie, and the devil loves to fill a person's head with lies, as he is the "father of lies."[3] Anytime Christians believe something contrary to the Bible, they are being deceived and lied to by a demonic spirit as the Holy Spirit is a "Spirit of truth."[4] If they believe that God does not love them, it is a lie. Anytime they believe that they cannot be forgiven, it is a lie. Anytime they believe that God has forsaken them, it is a lie. Anytime, they believe that they have been forgotten by God, it is a lie. Anytime they believe that God has given up on them, it is a lie. Anytime a person believes that life is hopeless, it is a lie. A person sincerely needs to have the ability to rightly discern the "the spirit of truth and the spirit of error."[5] Our thoughts need to be checked against the Bible to see if they are true or not and accept what the Bible says. In each of these two aforementioned cases, there was a stronghold that was demonic and that had taken over their minds and convinced them, contrary to what I quoted from Scripture to them, that their situation was hopeless as God had rejected them forever. God is always truth, as God "cannot lie."[6] If God spoke it to you, about you, and for you, then it is truth. Therefore, agree with God's Word and what it says about you and your situation.

Suicide

Suicide is a major problem in our society and results in thousands of deaths per year. According to the Centers for Disease Control and Prevention, the number of deaths in 2007 was 34,598.[7] Further, every fifteen minutes someone dies by suicide and it remains the eleventh leading cause of death in this country. Though suicide attempts are not reported, it is estimated that close to one million people make a suicide attempt each year.[8]

Suicide impacts a person's family, friends, coworkers, and community. In 2009, I had the unfortunate experience of grieving my best friend Rodger's suicide. Rodger was about twenty-five years older than I, but when he started working for the same social work agency, we became quickly attached. Rodger was a laid-back, easygoing person who truly cared about other people. His interactions with patients quickly earned their trust and fostered a good working relationship. Rodger was a person who opened his heart and home to me at a time when I was going through my divorce. Over several years, I became very close to him and his family.

Shortly before his death, Rodger began to experience increased anxiety and depression over his marriage possibly ending. He was sixteen years older than his wife, and he thought she was going to leave him. If she had left, he would have been alone and unable to start over because of his age. This subsequently led Rodger to start taking an antidepressant and an anti-anxiety medication. These medications did not seem to work, and he began telling friends he was having suicidal thoughts. Rodger kept his suicidal thoughts from me and then one night he just disappeared. Sadly, I received a call a few nights later—he was found dead from an overdose on alcohol and medications.

On the night we found out about Rodger's death, friends and family assembled together at his home to console his wife and family. We could not get past the questions of how and why. This situation seemed surreal. I specifically saw the pain on his wife's and children's faces and wish I could have taken it away from them. I am still connected with the family, and I see the struggles that they have with the emotions, blaming of each other and blaming of self. My friend was not just a statistic; he was a father, a husband, a friend, a coworker, a kindhearted and loving person, and a contributor to making this world a better place for the disadvantaged. Some may say that this was a selfish act, and partly it was, as he did not want to have to go through some dreaded changes in his life. However, from my standpoint, it was more of a self-focused or a self-centered act than a selfish act.

Roger's family is now dispersed about the country; the family ties have faded. Some do not speak to each other, one ended up in a psychiatric institution for threatening suicide, and another has threatened suicide.

When it comes to suicide, there are probably more questions than answers. I have had the opportunity to work with many people who have attempted suicide, and I was able to get information that was helpful regarding the reasons for the attempts. A few reasons were that the act was harming anyone else, that it was their life, and that they could do what they wanted. I know from personal experience that a person's act of suicide creates more harm to their loved ones than what they could imagine. I have seen the residual effects of the suicide of my best friend on his family and friends. It is possible that a child might attempt or commit suicide if a parent has attempted or committed suicide. But most would say that it is not the suicide of the parent that causes a teen's attempt at suicide, but the passed on biological illness of depression that is most likely the cause. But we cannot rule out that a child or teen is more likely to commit or attempt suicide if a parent attempts or commits suicide.

People may think that their life is their own and they can do what they want with it, such as committing suicide. But from a biblical standpoint that is simply not true. This is especially true for the Christian when they come into a relationship with Christ. When we enter into a life with Christ and receive Him as our Lord, our life is no longer our own. We live unto Christ, or through Christ toward God, and Christ lives in us. This automatically means that our life is ruled by what our Master Jesus said and by God's will. God's will for our lives does not include taking the very life that He has given us to live for Him.

THE BIBLE AND TREATMENT

Scriptures have a lot to say about believers taking care of themselves spiritually as well as physically. Taking care of our physical health could be eating right and exercising. The Bible has a lot to say about how a person is to eat. Likewise, individuals must take care of their physical health by seeking medical treatment for illness and disease, and this could include taking medications. This is evident when the Bible says, "He who is loose and slack in his work is brother to him who is a destroyer and he who does not use his endeavors to heal himself is brother to him who commits suicide"[9]

In the New Testament, the apostle Luke was called "the beloved physician"[10] and it is likely that Luke was not the only physician at that time. In Acts 27:14-44 Paul becomes shipwrecked. In Acts 28:8, after the shipwreck, Paul ends up on an island, Melita (Malta), where he lays his hands on a man named Publius, and he is healed. In the next verse, Acts 28:9, others from the island came and were healed as well. However, the word "healed" in verse 9 is a different Greek word than the one in verse 8 in Strong's Concordance. This could mean that the healing was done by medical means. It could have been Luke the physician involved in the healings with medicine on the island.

Hezekiah, king of Israel, becomes sick and is about to die. He prays and weeps before God who has mercy on him. God tells the prophet Isaiah that He heard Hezekiah's prayer and saw his tears and that he is going to heal Hezekiah. Isaiah then takes a "lump of figs"[11] and applies them to Hezekiah's boil after which he then "recovered" from the sickness of which he was going to die.

The "balm of Gilead"[12] is another medicine that is mentioned in Scripture. It is also mentioned in Genesis 37:25 where Joseph is sold into slavery. The "balm" is an ointment made from trees in the region of Gilead. We can deduce from Jeremiah 8:22 that the "balm of Gilead" was medicine: "Is there no balm in Gilead? Is there no physician there? Why then has not the health of the daughter of my people been restored?"[13] From a study on the "balm of Gilead" we find that "balm is used for a number of natural aromatic substances that are utilized for healing and soothing."[14]

Luke 10:34 explains how the Good Samaritan treated the wounds of the injured man by pouring "on oil and wine."[15] Wine in this case was being applied as an antiseptic, but it was also used as an anesthetic, relaxant, and tonic. In addition, olive oil prevents various cardiovascular diseases; it is also "rich in antioxidants" and helps people "suffering from various types of skin ailments."[16] Olive oil is a mild nonirritant and also used as an antibacterial agent. It might have also been applied to this injured man, as it keeps the skin hydrated and avoids infection.[17]

God is not against doctors or medications. In fact, Jesus said, "*It is not those who are well who need a physician, but those who are sick.*"[18] The Word of God is in agreement with the benefit of medications.

Therapy and medications can be successful in helping a person deal with and alleviate symptoms of depression. Further, it must be pointed out that if a person is severely depressed, medications can be beneficial in getting a person out of the depths of despair and hopelessness in order to benefit from other forms of treatment. But these "nonspiritual" methods do not deliver, heal, or set free a person from that depression. We cannot forget that our best hope of deliverance and freedom is found in Jesus Christ.

APOTHECARY (PHARMAKEIA)

I have had many people inpatient, on the psychiatric ward that refused to take medications due to their religious beliefs. I do not know what distinction they made between medications for a physical problem and medications for a psychiatric condition, but most of them still would take their physical health medications. I began pondering the different distinctions made between psychiatric medication and physical health medication following a message I heard preached on the word *pharmakeia*. Pharmakeia is the Greek word for "sorcery." I never heard this word up until about three years ago, so I began to research this word in Strong's Concordance.

In Acts 13:6 and 8, the word "sorcerer" actually means "magician" in the Greek. The King James Bible in Acts 8:11, the word "sorceries" is defined in the Greek as "magic." In Revelation 9:21 and 18:23 the word "sorcery" is *pharmakeia* in Greek. And in Revelation 21:8 and 22:15 "sorcerers" is *pharmakeus* in Greek. Interestingly enough, our word "pharmacy" is taken from the word *pharmakeia*. In the Old Testament, the King James Bible uses the word "witch"[19] who are those that "whisper a spell," "practice magic," or "use witchcraft."

It is interesting to find that these "sorcerers" or "witches" spoken about in the Bible were those who practiced magic or casted spells. They were those who would mix potions or medicate clients in order to send them into a state of mind to literally get them in touch with demons. There are drugs which are used in the medical field that produce psychoactive responses, but are to treat specific disorders and not to try and get someone in touch with the spirit world. People might abuse those medications specifically with those psychoactive properties, but that is not the intention of pharmaceutical companies or those prescribing them. Although our word "pharmacy" is taken from *pharmakeia*, there is likely not a connection between the demonology practices of the sorcerers or witches of the Bible and the modern-day pharmacists. It is also important to add that there is nothing specific in the Bible speaking against the taking of medications or going to see a physician. But the Bible does give specific guidelines for believers to "live by faith,"[20] which means our reliance is on Jesus as our healer.

JESUS THE HEALER

Jesus is the ultimate physician in whom there is no inability to heal, to deliver, or to set free. He is "the Lord that healeth thee,"[21] is translated *Yahweh Rapha*. If we look up the word "healeth" in Strong's Concordance, we find that it means "to cure," "to mend," or "to make whole." These meanings are also the same for the word "physician." This is further proof that "physicians" are good and were there to help a person who was ailing or sick or diseased. However, the meaning when applied to Jesus becomes different, as He is not fallible and heals not only the body but also the soul and spirit of man.

We see God's grace in Christ through the many examples of healing that Jesus and the disciples did, but also the healing that God is still performing today. Earthly physicians cannot be complete healers of the complete human, as there are parts of the human that are not from this earth. For example, God breathed life into man and made the body out of the earth. God made the whole person; the spirit of the man is something only God can heal, and man can heal only the physical body as God allows. We can see the fallacy or limitations of earthly healers in the well-known Bible story about the woman with the flow of blood (hemorrhage). There was "a woman, having a flow of blood for twelve years, who had spent all her livelihood on physicians and could not be healed by any."[22] She pushed her way through the crowd and touched Jesus' clothing, and "immediately her flow of blood stopped."[23] She could not be healed by any, but Jesus, who is the ultimate healer, showed up on the scene and completely delivered her from this hemorrhage. I love Jesus' words following the woman touching His clothing. He said, "Somebody touched Me, for I perceived power going out from Me."[24]

We conclude that the Bible is and must be our guide and foundation when it comes to issues that afflict us in our spirits, souls (mind, emotions, and will), and bodies. We must also realize that it must be our first source and have the final say in any situation we face in life. God's desire is to have us seek Him first for our problems and healing. This principle is expressed in the Old Testament regarding King Asa. "And, behold, the acts of Asa, first and last, lo, they are written in the book of the kings of Judah and Israel. And Asa in the thirty and ninth year of his reign was diseased in his feet, until his disease was exceeding great: yet in his disease he sought not to the Lord, but to the physicians."[25] It should be stressed again that God is not against doctors or medications. And individuals should seek a doctor if they have something going on with their body. However, they must seek God with their illnesses as well.

HEALING COMPASSION

One of the most disturbing tragedies of the present day is the disbelief of the majority of the body of Christ regarding the present-day ability and willingness of Jesus to heal. I have been privy to various views of Christians regarding the subject of healing, and these views create a divide within the church. This divide does not allow for the body of Christ to operate within the present-day healing ministry of Christ. Unfortunately, what is tragically missed by the proponents of the view that Jesus does not heal today is His overwhelming compassion for those in need. And Jesus desires "compassion."[26]

There are numerous examples of Scripture identifying Jesus' compassion just prior to His move to heal, to deliver, and to forgive. Jesus has an express desire to relieve us from whatever mess we are in, which is why He came. He not only shed His blood to save us on the cross but also demonstrated His compassion through His miraculous works of healings as well. The beauty of Jesus in terms of today is that His compassion continues to extend to us in our human condition of sickness, as He still desires to be part of our present-day lives. Many Scriptures portray the compassion of Jesus,[27] but the following Scriptures from Mark 1:40-42 express not only the compassion but also the willingness of Jesus to heal. "Now a leper came to Him, imploring

Him, kneeling down to Him, and saying to Him, 'If You are willing, You can make me clean.' Then Jesus, moved with compassion, stretched out His hand and touched Him, and said to Him, 'I am willing; be cleansed.' As soon as He had spoken, immediately the leprosy left him, and he was cleansed."[28] Jesus' unconditional love and compassion, which led Him to the cross, continues to be a present reality for our lives today. His actions, over two thousand years ago, continue its far-reaching compassion into today and bring us to the power of the cross of grace. As the "fullness of the Godhead bodily,"[29] Jesus is fully God and fully man. This allows Him insights into our humanity from the perception of our creator, but also into the weaknesses of humanity from first-hand experience. The humanity of Jesus allowed Him to connect to our humanity in all aspects of our needs.

Jesus' love and compassion manifest themselves through His works. His works showed that His compassion and love was active, but also led and continues to lead believers to the Father's heart. The Bible describes Jesus' works here on earth and is for today, and the Word is still alive and active. And Jesus Christ is the "same yesterday, today and forever."[30] Therefore, the Scriptures compel us to stand up and take notice about the subject of healing in its present-day capacity.

The scriptural contexts which declare for us to take notice are in Luke 7 and Mark 16. The greatest prophet in the Bible is John the Baptist, as he was the one who came just before Jesus to lay the groundwork for Jesus' ministry. John recognized Jesus as the "the Lamb of God, which taketh away the sin of the world"[31] It was this same John the Baptist, after being thrown in prison, who sent his disciples to Jesus in order to ask if He were the One for whom they waited. Jesus' response was awesome, as He responded by pointing to His works of healing and by telling them to not be offended in Him.

> And John calling unto him two of his disciples sent them to Jesus, saying, Art thou he that should come? or look we for another? When the men were come unto him, they said, John Baptist hath sent us unto thee, saying, Art thou he that should come? or look we for another? And in that same hour he cured many of their infirmities and plagues, and of evil spirits; and unto many that were blind he gave sight. Then Jesus

> answering said unto them, Go your way, and tell John
> what things ye have seen and heard; how that the blind
> see, the lame walk, the lepers are cleansed, the deaf hear,
> the dead are raised, to the poor the gospel is preached.
> And blessed is he, whosoever shall not be offended in
> me.[32]

We do not need to look for another; Jesus fulfills every need we have, and that includes healing.

The second set of Scripture is found in Mark 16. This set of Scripture is interesting because commanding the Jesus believer to lay hands on the sick, which would recover, leads a person to discover Jesus' present-day healing power and ministry. It is actually a command to a believer in this area of text. It is important to point out that Jesus is the one who commands in this area and the one who has the healing power.

> And he said unto them, Go ye into all the world, and
> preach the gospel to every creature. He that believeth
> and is baptized shall be saved; but he that believeth not
> shall be damned. And these signs shall follow them that
> believe; In my name shall they cast out devils; they shall
> speak with new tongues; They shall take up serpents; and
> if they drink any deadly thing, it shall not hurt them;
> they shall lay hands on the sick, and they shall recover.
> So then after the Lord had spoken unto them, he was
> received up into heaven, and sat on the right hand of
> God. And they went forth, and preached everywhere,
> the Lord working with them, and confirming the word
> with signs following. Amen.[33]

There are some interesting commands in this text that we need to pay close attention to. For one, "these signs shall follow them that believe" and "they shall lay hands on the sick, and they shall recover." Most importantly, the disciples obeyed this command, and God confirmed His word with the signs of miracles, signs, and wonders. And the set of Scripture is followed by the most important word, "Amen," which means "so be it." "So be it" for today that God continues to "confirm the word with signs following!"

Today, Jesus through the Bible and as the Living Word continues to point to His works of healings and miracles and tells us not to be offended in Him. Jesus is still working today with healing power, and it is up to us to maintain an accurate view of this present-day power. It beckons us to call and rely upon Him for the healing in our minds and bodies. The Word continues to be a reminder that God shed His compassion on us through Jesus and has good things for those who are His children.

Christians and the Placebo Effect

The "placebo affect" is important for us to dissect, as the person's faith that a treatment will work appears to be the necessary catalyst for the expected change. Faith is the presupposition that something will work. In the Christian experience, faith is the necessary catalyst that brings the result which that person expects. Christians from a biblical perspective receive all things by faith from the very beginning of their walk with God. Essentially, when they hear the gospel and put their faith into it being true, they get a result. That result is forgiveness of sins, being made right with God, or salvation as most call it. This faith makes the power of God become an active agent in their life to bring the expected result of salvation.

This principle of believing in the Word of God and receiving from the Word of God is important to Christians. In essence, they apply their faith to God and His Words and then God's Word become effective in their lives. This faith that a person places in medications or a placebo working for them is the same faith which will work when placed into the Word of God for hope, healing, and deliverance; and the Word of God is never fallible. Proverbs 4:20-22 states, "My son, pay attention to what I say; listen closely to my words. Do not let them out of your sight, keep them within your heart; for they are life to those who find them and health to a man's whole body."[34] According to Strong's Concordance 4832, the word "health" in Hebrew means "curative, a medicine, a cure, or deliverance." The faith we can put into the Word of God is a "medicine" for any problem that we have going on in our life.

So the Word of God is like "medicine" when we apply it to the situation. We apply this word by finding what is says about our situation, holding fast to that word, and then relying on it to change that situation. Initially, we must come to God with faith, so that when we apply the Word of God to an area of our life where there is a need, it will change that area. When you believe that the Word of God is alive, is active, is for today, and it applies to your situation, then you will "know the truth, and the truth will make you free."[35]

CHAPTER THREE

FOUNDATION

FOR A PERSON BUILDING A house, the most important factor is a solid foundation. For athletes of today to perform at the top of their game, they need to have a strong body core. Likewise, for Christians to function in their lives, there is a need for a strong foundation that is built upon God. This foundation can be achieved only by having a life built upon Jesus Christ, the Rock. Building a life upon Jesus and through Jesus to God is the most essential part of the life that we are trying to build, as Jesus is the "chief corner stone."[1] Further, "in Him we live and move and exist, as even some of your own poets have said, 'For we also are His children.'"[2] Additional foundational principles for a life built upon God must include an understanding and reliance upon God's Word (Jesus is the living word) and a daily relationship with God in Christ. Salvation, the Bible, and a relationship with God are the foundational truths a depressed person must have in life to have an anchor for the soul in the middle of the battle with depression. This foundation of salvation and the truth from the Word of God cannot be removed by any sickness or disease, and that includes depression.

JESUS IN THE PROCESS

If Jesus is the "bread of life,"[3] if He is the one who came to give us "life, and have it abundantly,"[4] and if He is the one who came to "bind up the broken hearted,"[5] where is He in the midst of our struggles? If God loves me so much and sent Jesus to die for me, why did He do this to me? These are some of the questions that people might ask in the midst of their circumstances. These may be the questions we ourselves have asked at one point in time. These are okay questions to ask and difficult to answer, but if believers focus on these questions, they miss the greatest work Jesus has ever done. As aforementioned in the previous paragraph, salvation is the most important foundation in a person's life. Salvation is the most important foundation for everyone, but we know that not all people will receive the truth about the death, burial, and resurrection (gospel) of Jesus Christ. If a person has Jesus and is depressed, he or she is in better standing than someone who is depressed without Jesus. Jesus, in John 6, accentuates the level of importance of salvation in a person's life.

JOHN 6

Jesus is the only one who can save us from our sins and truly give us life, as He is the "bread of life"[6] and as "man shall not live on bread alone."[7] I really enjoy the account in the Gospels about the feeding of the multitude. It is actually told in all four of the gospels, but John accentuates clearly the importance in the text of Scripture. To summarize this account in the Scriptures, Jesus just heard from the disciples all they had done and had taught, and He wanted them to get away to rest for awhile. Multitudes of people followed Jesus and the disciples, and they could not get away from them. They were in a deserted place. Jesus taught the multitude many truths there, and they listened to Him all day late into the day. Jesus wanted the disciples to feed them, and the only food found was a boy's dinner of "five loaves and two fish."[8] Jesus made this little boy's meal more than enough to feed the five thousand. Not only did Jesus feed them, but there were "twelve full baskets"[9] left over. Mark 6:34 sums up, in part, why Jesus did the things He did in the feeding of the multitude: "Jesus, when He came out, saw a great multitude and was moved with compassion for them, because they were like sheep not having a shepherd."[10] Without Jesus as a person's shepherd, people are truly lost even though they may have found food for their body. If we read a little further into John 6, we can see that Jesus' main point was providing for our salvation with His body and His blood. "Jesus said to them, 'I am the bread of life; he who comes to Me will not hunger, and he who believes in Me will never thirst.'"[11] "For this is the will of My Father, that everyone who beholds the Son and believes in Him will have eternal life, and I Myself will raise him up on the last day"[12]

THE WORD OF GOD

The love of God has been established in the Bible and fully expressed in the person of Jesus Christ. John 3:16 reveals this love: "For God so loved the world, that He gave His only begotten Son, that whoever believes in Him shall not perish, but have eternal life." Further, in Romans 8:38-39, the Holy Spirit reveals, "For I am persuaded that neither death nor life, nor angels nor principalities nor powers, nor things present nor things to come, nor height nor depth, nor any other created thing, shall be able to separate us from the love of God which is in Christ Jesus our Lord."[13]

There are countless other passages that reveal God's love for us. The point that I am trying to get across is that if we never open our Bible or have someone open the Bible and preach God's love to us, we would never know about His love for us. A person, therefore, cannot have a solid foundation where there is no knowledge with understanding. Hosea 4:6 explains best what happens when people do not know the commandment or what God has to say on a matter: "My people are destroyed for lack of knowledge. Because you have rejected knowledge, I also will reject you from being my priest. Since you have forgotten the law of your God, I also will forget your children."

The burden to obtain and follow knowledge is on each of us individually.

It is important to know where the promises of God are for us in terms of the issues that we face in life. As mentioned earlier, if we do not know what is written, it is easy for the enemy to deceive us in that area. John 10:10 gives the full explanation to the enemy's tactics: "The thief comes only to steal and kill and destroy; I came that they may have life, and have it abundantly." One of the tactics of the enemy is to steal the Word of God from us. In the parable of the sower, God uses a farmer sowing seed into various types of soil to represent the Word of God that is being preached to people and the various conditions of their heart in receiving the Bible. Jesus explains the parable:

> This is the meaning of the parable: The seed is the word
> of God. Those along the path are the ones who hear,
> and then the devil comes and takes away the word from
> their hearts, so that they may not believe and be saved.
> Those on the rock are the ones who receive the word
> with joy when they hear it, but they have no root. They
> believe for a while, but in the time of testing they fall
> away. The seed that fell among thorns stands for those
> who hear, but as they go on their way they are choked
> by life's worries, riches and pleasures, and they do not
> mature. But the seed on good soil stands for those with
> a noble and good heart, who hear the word, retain it,
> and by persevering produce a crop.[14]

The Word of God is powerful. It is a seed that grows in us as we walk
with God and feed it. It is something we have to receive and stand on
(preserve it), which is a condition of the heart, but we do have to realize
that we have an enemy who does not want us to have that Word.

From the very beginning, God used His words to create the heavens
and the earth. It was from the very beginning that His word had
authority. Not all people's words have authority. A person may speak a
word and yet can never bring it to fruition. Therefore, a man is only as
good as his word that he can carry out. Similarly, God's word is only
as good as He is. Unlike man, all of God's word has authority. He can
back it up and perform whatever He says. We can see this from the
beginning in Genesis when God said, "Let there be," and there was.
God says in Isaiah 55:10-11,

> For as the rain and the snow come down from heaven,
> And do not return there without watering the earth
> And making it bear and sprout, And furnishing seed to
> the sower and bread to the eater; So will My word be
> which goes forth from My mouth; It will not return to
> Me empty, Without accomplishing what I desire, And
> without succeeding in the matter for which I sent it.

Just so we do not get confused, the Bible lets us know from where the
Word of God comes. First it comes from above. Second, it comes from

"God's mouth." Many people think that it is only inspired word, written by man and therefore only good advice, fallible and not to be trusted. But this verse clears this misunderstanding up, and 2 Timothy 3:16 reminds us that "all Scripture is given by inspiration of God,"[15] even though it is written by man. The conclusion is that the Word of God has to be the center in our lives, and it must be our foundation, as it is the only foundation that will not crumble.

RELATIONSHIPS

Relationships are an important part of our healing process. One symptom of depression or other mental illnesses is that they tend to create a distance and separation from people. This separation could include the thought that no one wants us around or that nobody loves us or that no one understands us. Depression also has a significant component of feelings of worthlessness, low motivation, isolation, low energy, and apathy that leads us to stay away from others. Essentially, we are cut off from family, from friends, and from our community. If we are depressed, relationships can be a source of strength, connectedness to other humans, and purpose.

This reminds me of a man who came on a fishing trip with me and other men from church. This man told us about his life and what was going on. He was diagnosed with bipolar disorder and tended to be more on the depressed side. He let us know that his depression had been so bad that he was not leaving his basement, interacting much with his wife, or really doing much with his kids. He stated that he had been contemplating suicide. For some reason, he came on this trip with these men, and something happened with him. This man found connection with others, and he explained to us that he did not know that there were so many good Christian men out there. It appears that the enemy had got him alone and was lying about relationships and the importance of them. Relationships keep us connected with others, specifically other believers who can strengthen and encourage us. The light was shed on the enemy's lie about relationships and other Christians being hypocrites, and led this man to have hope as well as getting rid of this idea about taking his own life.

Relationships from a biblical standpoint are crucial. God, from the beginning, created man to be in relationship with Him. God came down and spent time with man (Adam and Eve) in the Garden of Eden. Man, unfortunately, destroyed this intimacy with God by sinning and breaking the covenant. However, thank God, Christ reconciled us back into relationship with Him and washed away the sin that separated us from God. Through Christ, we have "been adopted"[16] into God's family and are "heirs of God, and joint-heirs with Christ."[17] As adopted children, we can call God our Father. This is another relational term that we can call God when we are in His family. When we have people in our lives, we call them friends. Jesus also talks about this concept in that He says, "No longer do I call you slaves, for the slave does not know what his master is doing; but I have called you friends."[18]

Man was not only created for relationship with God, but he was also created for relationship with one another. The Bible makes this point in that a "cord of three *strands* is not quickly torn apart."[19] Further, if a man is alone and falls, how can someone pick him up and get him back on the right track? If he has a friend, this friend can see him fall and pick him back up again. It is interesting how God brings these people into our lives to help us and provide us what we need from a flesh-and-blood body. However, God also provided a way for us to never be alone and it was in Christ as "God was manifested in the flesh."[20] In doing so, He shows that He is a personal God who took part in our sufferings, in order to reconcile us and to have relationship with us. God deeply wants us to have a relationship with Him and has struck, not a contract, but a covenant relationship with us. He wants us to love others as well.

GOD'S PROMISE OF ABIDING WITH US . . . RELATIONSHIP

Jesus said to abide "in Him" because He is the one who sustains us and the very source of our lives. Some may question His abiding with them in the midst of the darkness of depression. It might feel like God is far during that time. It may literally feel as if God has forsaken the depressed person. A few Scriptures show God's heart regarding His never leaving us nor forsaking us no matter what is going on. We can be reassured by them that God has not left us, and hears our cries.

First, let us take a look at Romans 8:39, where the Bible says that there is nothing that "will be able to separate us from the love of God, which is in Christ Jesus our Lord." Even in the midst of whatever we have going on, Jesus will be there beside us as he said: "I will never leave you nor forsake you."[21] John 10:29-30 says, "My Father, who has given them to Me, is greater than all; and no one is able to snatch them out of My Father's hand. I and my Father are one." In Psalm 139:7-10, the psalmist says, "Where can I go from Your Spirit? Or where can I flee from Your presence? If I ascend into heaven, You are there; if I make my bed in hell, behold, You are there. If I take the wings of the morning and dwell in the uttermost parts of the sea, Even there Your hand shall lead me, and Your right hand shall hold me."[22] These are just a few of the Scriptures that show God's thoughts and feelings toward us.

God is always abiding with us, as His Spirit is always with us. Jesus says, "I will ask the Father, and He will give you another Helper, that He may be with you forever."[23] This verse is saying that the Father sends us a comforter, the Holy Spirit, because "He," the Father, wants to abide with us forever. Jesus talks about this comforter coming who would be sent in His name. Jesus further expounds on this wonderful news of a comforter when He says, "The Spirit of truth, whom the world cannot receive, because it does not see Him or know Him, *but* you know Him because He abides with you and will be in you. I will not leave you as orphans; I will come to you."[24] The Bible frequently uses another word for "orphans," and that word is "fatherless." Jesus' promise is that He himself "will come" so as to not leave us fatherless.

ABIDING WITH GOD IN RELATIONSHIP

God is not looking for part-time relationships with Him. In fact, He told us to "love the LORD your God with all your heart, with all your soul, and with all your strength."[25] This means that He is requiring a deep and intimate relationship with Him. This is more than giving Him mere lip service or attending church a few days a week. In fact, Jesus said "Hypocrites! Well did Isaiah prophesy about you, saying: These people draw near to Me with their mouth, and honor Me with *their* lips, But their heart is far from Me."[26] These same people exist today, people only wanting the benefits of a relationship with God without the intimacy. Simply put, it is really about knowing who God is. We get to know someone through an intimate and close relationship. There is something more that God desires from us, and I believe that to be "abiding in him."

Jesus says in John 15:8, "I am the vine, you are the branches." This Scripture is talking about abiding "in Him." This statement "in Him" means a very close fellowship and deep relationship with God through Jesus Christ our Lord. Jesus says in verse 7, "If you abide in Me, and My words abide in you, you will ask what you desire, and it shall be done for you." This is a promise from Jesus Himself, which we will receive when we abide in that close, deep, and intimate relationship with Him. He says, "My words abide in you," meaning that we must obey His words, have them set in our heart, and apply them in our lives. I know people who do not see a prayer answered, as they only go to God when they have a problem, need a healing, need deliverance, or have a need in their life. This is not abiding in God.

Psalm 91:9-16 sums up this close relationship we have with God. This set of Scriptures says,

> If you make the Most High your dwelling, even the Lord, who is my refuge—then no harm will befall you, no disaster shall come near your tent. For he will command his angels concerning you to guard you in all your ways; they will lift you up in their hands, so that you will not strike your foot against a stone. You will tread upon the lion and the cobra; you will trample the great lion and the serpent. "Because he loves me," says the Lord, "I will rescue him; I will protect him, for he acknowledges my name. He will call upon me, and I will answer him; I will be with him in trouble, I will deliver him and honor him. With long life I will satisfy him and show him my salvation."[27]

In the aforementioned Scriptures, when we "make the Most High" our "dwelling" or when we "abide in Him," the promise of God to answer our prayers is fulfilled. Most people I know, even myself, have focused on Psalm 91:10-12, pertaining to God's protection, but the real focus should be on verse 9 where we make God our dwelling place. If we make God our dwelling place, then we tap into the source from where everything flows. When we make God our focus, then this is what happens: "Because he has set his love upon Me, therefore I will deliver him; I will set him on high, because he has known My name. He shall call upon Me, and I will answer him; I will be with him in trouble; I will deliver him and honor him. With long life I will satisfy him, And show him My salvation." The importance of this section of Scriptures is that this is God speaking about David or us. This set of Scriptures is a place into which we can actually insert our name. For example, if I put my name into this text it would look like this: "Because he (Derrin) has set his love upon Me, therefore I will deliver him; I will set him (Derrin) on high, because he has known My name. He (Derrin) shall call upon Me, and I will answer him; I will be with him (Derrin) in trouble; I will deliver him (Derrin) and honor him. With long life I will satisfy him (Derrin), and show him My salvation."

CHAPTER FOUR

KNOW YOUR IDENTITY IN CHRIST

MANY PEOPLE STRUGGLE WITH THEIR identity in this world. There are many teens and young adults trying to find their identity by our culture. Others have their identities wrapped up in work. For men, this is an important topic, as men often develop their identities based on what kind of work they do. If men are in conversation with one another, the question about what they do for a living is soon to come up. Most men get lost if they lose their employment, as they do not know their identity any longer.

Many Christians, including myself, also struggle with our identity as defined by the Bible. We may identify ourselves as a Christian or as a follower of Jesus without truly knowing our identity in Him. Without knowing our identity, our walk with God will be more difficult, as the enemy will try and make us question our identity. He does this to not only discredit God, but to make us stumble. If he can get us mixed up in our head about our identity, he can potentially defeat us with our own mind. Our identification is extremely important in the battle against the devil and in maintaining our peace. The devil knows that this is important. So he will try and steal our identity. No set of Scriptures is clearer about the devil's intentions to get us to question our identity than Matthew 4:1-11. Shortly after Jesus' baptism, He is led away by the Holy Spirit into the desert. There Jesus fasts for forty days and forty nights. It is after these forty days of fasting that the devil picks his opportunity to try and tempt Jesus. The devil engages Jesus in conversation, and each time he leads with the same statement, "if you are the Son of God." This is an attempt on his part to try and get Jesus to question His identity as the Son of God. The devil and the demons know who the Son of God is, but the devil attempts to get Jesus to question his position as the Son of God anyway. The devil is bold enough to question our identity as a child of God in Christ as well. Despite the devil's attempts, we are God's children.

Depression often leaves us with thoughts and feelings that we are worthless or unlovable. Our natural view of how we see ourselves is clouded by past experiences. Knowing who we are in Christ helps us to see ourselves as God sees us, instead of looking at ourselves through our own perceptions. God sees us much differently; He sees you as His special treasure.[1]

Many Christians are living a miserable life in spite of all the blessings they have as a result of their identity in Christ. They feel bad about themselves in terms of their past and continue to live in bondage to those things. They do not see themselves through the eyes of Christ. We need to realize that God has special plans for us and that we are worth something to Him. Jeremiah 29:11 says, "For I know the thoughts I think toward you, says the Lord, thoughts of peace and not of evil, to give you a future and a hope."[2] I heard it said this way: "God created your purpose and then created you to fit that purpose." You have a uniqueness all your own, and He created you to fit your purpose. "For we are His workmanship created in Christ Jesus for good works, which God prepare beforehand that we would walk in them."[3]

Remember Moses and Gideon? They saw themselves as incapable, but God saw more. He saw Moses as the one to deliver the Israelites and Gideon as a mighty man of valor. Another example of how God sees us in the Bible is Paul. Prior to being transformed in Christ, Paul (then Saul) was a persecutor and murderer of the Christians. This did not stop God from using Him. God changed Saul's name to Paul, and Paul became a new creation in Christ. His former self had passed away, and all things were made new.[4] Think of how different Paul's story would have been if he had continued to only see himself as a murderer of Christians instead of taking on his new identity in Christ. Of course, we would not have a lot of the New Testament to read. Paul not only saw himself in Christ but also was an exhorter of the brethren, so his speech was not of his old self either. God made you, made a way to save you, and waited for you! God has never turned His back on you. He has seen the most rotten things you have ever done in your life, and He still loves you. Get into the Word to see how special you are in Him. "You did not choose Me but I chose you, and appointed you that you would go and bear fruit, and *that* your fruit would remain, so that whatever you ask of the Father in My name He may give to you."[5]

I recall one morning I was praying and received a fresh revelation of who I was in Him and how much God loved me. I started thinking about God's love for us. I realized that God had seen the worst of the worst of my sin and still loved me! He not only still loved me but also waited for me to return to Him! God doesn't turn His back to us or give up on us. He wants you to be a child of the Most High God and be adopted into *His family.* When you are a Christian and have accepted Christ as your Savior, you are a new person on the inside. You then need to focus on the one who saved you. As you focus on the one who saved you, let your mind be renewed by the Word of God. Alter your perception; recreate it in reality, based on God's Word about who you are in Him; let your "old man" pass away; and live out of the "new creature"[6] God has made you in Christ.

IDENTIFICATION THROUGH NAMES

God is a God who reveals Himself by His name, thereby establishing His glory, power, and character. When He came to Moses and wanted him to deliver His people from Egypt, God identified Himself by "the God of your father, the God of Abraham, the God of Isaac, and the God of Jacob."[7] This meant something specific to Moses, and this declaration from God put fear in Moses. The reason was that through the names of "Abraham, Isaac, and Jacob," the promises to them were established, and these were passed on to their generation.

> Then Moses said to God, "Behold, I am going to the sons of Israel, and I will say to them, 'The God of your fathers has sent me to you.' Now they may say to me, 'What is His name?' What shall I say to them?" God said to Moses, "I AM WHO I AM"; and He said, "Thus you shall say to the sons of Israel, 'I AM has sent me to you.'" God, furthermore, said to Moses, "Thus you shall say to the sons of Israel, 'The Lord, the God of your fathers, the God of Abraham, the God of Isaac, and the God of Jacob, has sent me to you.' This is My

name forever, and this is My memorial-name to all generations."[8]

This name that God revealed to them, that was to all generations, was Yahweh, and it was the same revealed name in Jesus. Jesus means "Yahweh saves." Also, Jesus said, "before Abraham was, I AM,"[9] making himself that same one God who revealed himself to Moses in the Old Testament. This is the importance of the name of Jesus and why it caused so much controversy back then, and why it causes so much controversy now.

Names are extremely important in the Bible and carry a lot of meaning. The Bible gives a lot of accounts in which God would establish something by His name, and "He could swear by no one greater."[10] We can see that names are important throughout the whole Bible, especially the name of Jesus. Mary and Joseph were told to name the child Jesus because He would save His people. This name is important because Jesus means "Yahweh saves." Jesus is the "name which is above every name,"[11] and there is "no other name under heaven that has been given among men by which we must be saved."[12] Jesus identified Himself with this name and with His Father who had named Him. Jesus said to the Father, "glorify Your name," and the Father said, "I have both glorified it, and will glorify it again."[13]

The apostles identified with this name of Jesus as well, and were beaten and told not to preach in this name. It was imperative for the rulers of that day to prevent people from believing in the name of Jesus. In Acts 3, Peter and John healed a man, lame from his mother's womb, by the name of Jesus. Peter said to this lame man, "In the name of Jesus Christ the Nazarene—walk!"[14] This resulted in the lame man being completely healed and "walking and leaping and praising God."[15] You would think that people would be praising God, but there were many who were not, and Peter and John were taken into custody by the religious leaders. The religious leaders demanded to know "by what power, or in what name, have you done this?"[16] Peter and John went on to explain that it was by the authority of the name of Jesus that they had done this. Later in the account of this interaction with the leaders of the religious establishments of that day, we find that the leaders threatened them to not speak in that name of Jesus any longer.[17] We can deduce from the Scriptures that God's name causes controversy and that where that name is, there is power. Where He chooses to put His name and on whom He chooses to put His name, there is power. We also find that this "name which is above every name"[18] is still a name that causes controversy today. But for those of us who are saved, this name is wonderful.

JESUS GIVES US A NEW NAME

Throughout the Scripture, we see that God changed Abram's name to Abraham, as there was significant meaning to it. Abraham means "father of a multitude." We see that God did this although Abraham had no kids at that time; but the promises were in that new name, and Abraham started to declare that name.

We read about another significant name change: Saul to Paul. Saul, before he became Paul and impacted the world with the gospel, was a murderer of Christians. However, he received a new name and did great works with the new name.

Likewise, we not only have been given the highest name, the name of Jesus with whom we identify, but I believe we also have a new name given to us by God. We are no longer to identify with the workings of that old sinful man we once were.

Jesus is says in Revelation 2:17, "He who has an ear, let him hear what the Spirit says to the churches. To him who overcomes, to him I will give *some* of the hidden manna, and I will give him a white stone, and a new name written on the stone which no one knows but he who receives it."[19] Jesus has stored up for us a new name. Jesus makes us a new person and gives us a new identity; we are to have our identity in Him, and He will give us a new name in heaven. Jesus probably already sees us according to that new name! And when we take on our new identity in Christ Jesus, we are taking on the identity of the new name He has in store for us.

The reason I have gone into such depth about our identity with those names is because God has chosen us Christians to put His name on us. When we take on the name of Jesus, we put on Jesus Christ and become a new person. Therefore, we need to begin to identify ourselves with Him and realize the power that the name of Jesus has in our lives. Further, if God has chosen to put the name of Jesus on us, that is also where His blessings reside as well as His promises. The new person that we are and are becoming is what we need to focus on. We need to start living up to our new identity and new name. We do that is by learning and knowing who we are in Jesus Christ. Someday God will change our names in order to not identify with any past names as well as with the terrible things we did in that name. That is probably also why He puts His name on us, to become our new identity.

RENEWING YOUR MIND

Depression has a self-perpetuating nature to it. When a down mood presents itself, it will bring negative thoughts with it. The down mood perpetuates negative thinking, and these thoughts tend to continue in that negative pattern. The more we focus on how poorly we feel and how miserable our circumstances are, the worse things can become with our mood.

Our mind has to go through a process of reshaping from its former perceptions and beliefs. This is where the Bible comes in. The Bible is the source for renewing our mind especially from the way negative experiences and the world have shaped it. Romans 12:2 gives a clear picture of what this means:

> Do not be conformed to this world (this age), [fashioned after and adapted to its external, superficial customs], but be transformed (changed) by the [entire] renewal of your mind [by its new ideals and its new attitude], so that you may prove [for yourselves] what is the good and acceptable and perfect will of God, even the thing which is good and acceptable and perfect [in His sight for you].[20]

When we are called by God out of the world culture, system, and ideals, He wants to change our mind and conform it to His mind. He does this because He wants us to connect with Him more and think biblically in our perceptions. He wants to cleanse us of the negative and ungodly thought patterns which inhibit us from knowing Him. He wants us to rely on Him, take Him at His Word, and make it a focus of our lives. Jeremiah 15:16 says, "Your words were found and I ate them, and your words became for me a joy and the delight of my heart; for I have been called by your name, O LORD God of hosts."[21] When we are called by His name, His Word brings peace and stability in our thought life. God's Word says, "Your word is a lamp to my feet and a light to my path."[22] It also says, "Those who love your law have great peace, and nothing causes them to stumble."[23] Depression causes us to meditate on negativity. But we need to meditate on that which is good. According to 2 Corinthians10:4-5, we need to pull "down strongholds, casting down arguments and every high thing that exalts itself against the knowledge of God, bringing every thought into captivity to the obedience of Christ."[24] To counter this negativity, meditation should be on God's Word. Joshua 1:8 tells us, "This Book of the Law shall not depart from your mouth, but you shall meditate on it day and night, so that you may be careful to do according to all that is written in it."[25] To meditate means to engage in a thought or contemplation. It is to have a thought in your mind on purpose. To break these strongholds, we need to purposely renew our minds by purposely meditating on God's words. During this process, we will fight against feelings and the devil. But we can gain the victory if we continue to set our eyes on God and get His words in our hearts.

SET YOUR MIND ON THINGS ABOVE

Renewing your mind can be a difficult task, but it is essential if you want to keep your thoughts focused on something other than your past mistakes and failures leading to a misperceived weakened bond with God. The difficulty is taking the proper course to renewing your mind. We have already established that we need to renew our mind by the Word of God solely, so that is a good place to start. A key component to living with a renewed mind is forgetting our old self and bringing to remembrance what the Bible says about us as a new man. We "put on" this new man by renewing the spirit on our minds. Ephesians 4:20-24 says it this way:

> But you have not so learned Christ, if indeed you have
> heard Him and have been taught by Him, as the truth

41

is in Jesus: that you put off, concerning your former conduct, the old man which grows corrupt according to the deceitful lusts, and be renewed in the spirit of your mind, and that you put on the new man which was created according to God, in true righteousness and holiness.[26]

We renew this spirit on our mind, thus putting on the new man we are created in Christ. We can put on this new man by renewing our mind, which can be done by meditating on "whatever things are true, whatever things are noble, whatever things are just, whatever things are pure, whatever things are lovely, whatever things are of good report, if there is any virtue and if there is anything praiseworthy."[27] We can set our mind on the things above by continually enacting spiritual disciplines. These following spiritual disciplines seek God through prayer,[28] read and meditate on the Bible, [29] fellowship with spiritually sound people who are encouraging, and remain in a state of thankfulness and praise to God.[30]

CHAPTER FIVE

RIGHTEOUSNESS

ONE OF OUR POSITIONS IN Christ, as His beloved and His accepted, is righteousness. This area seems to be a struggle for Christians, as they see themselves through their shortcomings. They do not realize the right standing they have with God, and if they do commit sin, they beat themselves up about it. This can lead to an emotional roller coaster without peace of mind with God. These ways of thinking can lead them to be depressed, as somehow they have failed God.

It must be reiterated that we live in a physical body and are all susceptible to sin. Paul expounds on this truth in Romans 7:18, "For I know that nothing good dwells in me, that is, in my flesh; for the willing is present in me, but the doing of the good *is* not."[1] Our spirit man is saved, but our flesh or natural man is not saved. Our flesh will not actually be redeemed until Jesus comes. The Bible refers to our spirit as the inner man. Paul tells the Ephesians "that He would grant you, according to the riches of His glory, to be strengthened with power through His Spirit in the inner man."[2] We do not condone sin, and we should not sin and abuse the grace we have in God. Romans says it this way: "What shall we say then? Are we to continue in sin so that grace may increase? May it never be! How shall we who died to sin still live in it?"[3] The Bible lets us know that our spirit should bring our flesh into subjection as well as we should rule over sin. Paul wrote, "But I discipline my body and make it my slave, so that, after I have preached to others, I myself will not be disqualified."[4] Paul is saying that his spirit or inner man needs to rule over his flesh that is not saved. The other area that discusses our rule over sin is in Genesis. Cain's sacrifice was rejected by God, and Cain became angry. God spoke to Cain and told him, "Why are you angry? And why has your countenance fallen? If you do well, will not your countenance be lifted up? And if you do not do well, sin is crouching at the door; and its desire is for you, but you must master it."[5] We know that Cain did not rule over sin but let sin rule over him and went and killed his brother.

People might read through this part of the Scripture and disagree and give Scriptures in the Bible that seem contrary to the statement that we could be righteous before God. These Scriptures are usually Psalm 53:1-3 and reiterated in the New Testament in Romans 3:9-18. The psalmist penned,

> The fool has said in his heart, "There is no God," They are corrupt, and have committed abominable injustice; There is no one who does good. God has looked down from heaven upon the sons of men To see if there is anyone who understands, Who seeks after God. Every one of them has turned aside; together they have become corrupt; there is no one who does good, not even one.[6]

Essentially, these two Scriptures are stating man's position of unrighteousness before he is saved as man is not righteous in his own standing and is in need of a Savior.

THE LORD OUR RIGHTEOUSNESS

We discussed earlier in the book how the name of God, *Yahweh Rapha*, shows that He is our healer. In same way that this name is revealed so we could put our trust in God in the area for healing, so the name *Yahweh Tsidkenu* is revealed so we can put our trust in God for righteousness. The name *Yahweh Tsidkenu* was given in the Old Testament and revealed in Jesus in the New Testament. In the book of Jeremiah, it says, "'Behold, the days are coming,' says the Lord, 'That I will raise to David a Branch of righteousness; A King shall reign and prosper, And execute judgment and righteousness in the earth. In His days Judah will be saved, And Israel will dwell safely; Now this is His name by which He will be called: The Lord Our Righteousness.'"[7] Jesus is that "Branch of righteousness." In other words, Jesus is the source or the root from where we get our righteousness. Jesus in the book of John says, "I am the vine, you are the branches. He who abides in Me, and I in him, bears much fruit; for without Me you can do nothing. If anyone does not abide in Me, he is cast out as a branch and is withered; and they gather them and throw them into the fire, and they are burned."[8] Paul says, "For if the firstfruit is holy, the lump is also holy; and if the root is holy, so are the branches. And if some of the branches were broken off, and you, being a wild olive tree, were grafted in among them, and with them became a partaker of the root and fatness of the olive tree, do not boast against the branches. But if you do boast, remember that you do not support the root, but the root supports you."[9] I used this set of Scriptures to point out that we are "grafted" into Christ; He is the "root" that supports us, and if "the root is holy [Jesus]," then so are we. "Holy" means "pure" or "blameless" in the Bible. It means that we are blameless before God or in right standing with Him . . . righteous. We can still sin as a Christian, but the truth is God is no longer angry with our sin as He took all that anger out on Jesus when He was on the cross. He might correct and discipline us for sinning, as He wants us in obedience to Him, but He is no longer angry with us when we do sin.

To bring this point home that we can be righteous before God when we are saved, we will turn to Jesus' death on the cross. Let us take a look at the cross where Jesus became sin so we could have His righteousness. There was some type of exchange between Jesus and man upon that cross. That exchange was Jesus' righteousness for our sins. Only by what Jesus did on the cross could we be righteous before God. Isaiah 53:4-12 gives beautiful details about Jesus taking our sins, iniquities, and transgressions. But the following Scripture in the New Testament describes exactly what happened to Jesus on the cross and the reason why it happened. "For He made Him who knew no sin to be sin for us, that we might become the righteousness of God in Him."[10] Jesus was actually made sin so we could be righteous. We can now be righteous by what Jesus has done.

CHAPTER SIX

UNFORGIVINGNESS

I LOVE TO FACILITATE A group at work called "Old Emotional Baggage." It addresses the experiences from people's past that impact their current life. These experiences could also impact their relationship with God. The "old emotional baggage" could be regret, childhood abuse, anger, death, divorce, relationships, and so forth. I have found that people have many wounds and hurts from the past that are currently impacting their lives and do not allow them the peace and joy they so desperately want. It amazes me that most people can easily identify their old emotional baggage and get very specific, but they cannot let it go. Their attention to detail is quite remarkable, as they remember not only what was done but also what was said.

None of us are immune to past hurts, pains, and wounds. We all have experienced them. But it is easier to realize when we are being wounded and not so easy when we are wounding others. It is very easy to do something that could wound others because we are human and will fall short and make mistakes. This area of being fallible and making mistakes as humans is one area that we need to be aware of when it comes to recognizing and forgiving other people's mistakes. In my experience, most people want to hold on to hurts and offenses. What God got across to me regarding unforgivingness is that if we deal with situations from our flesh, it is easy to hold on to unforgivingness, as the flesh naturally wants to hold on to wrongs or offenses. The Bible talks a lot about living by our flesh and by the spirit. Our flesh does not know God, but our spirit does. Our spirit can be guided by God, but our flesh needs to be brought into subjection by our spirit. Forgiveness is natural to do when we walk by the Spirit of God and do not live according to the flesh.[1] It is only when we are spiritually minded that we realize the importance of forgiveness, and only by the Spirit of God do we walk out this forgiveness in all situations. In essence, what is going on here is the battle between the flesh and the spirit. The following Scripture sums this up: "I say then: Walk in the Spirit, and you shall not fulfill the lust of the flesh. For the flesh lusts against the Spirit, and the Spirit against the flesh; and these are contrary to one another, so that you do not do the things that you wish."[2] If we obey the Spirit, we will walk in forgiveness. When it comes to forgiveness, God holds us to a higher standard. In Matthew 18, "Peter came and said to Him, "Lord, how often shall my brother sin against me and I forgive him? Up to seven times?"[3] This was most likely a sincere question on Peter's part, as the spiritual leaders of that day believed that if people did something more than seven times, it meant they were not really sorry and should not be forgiven. Peter may have thought that his standard of seven times was a great standard, and a sense of pride crept in. However, Jesus held Peter to a higher standard and replied, "I do not say to you, up to seven times, but up to seventy times seven."[4] Essentially, there is no limit to how much we forgive someone, as there is no limit with God in forgiveness of us.

When we look at Jesus, we can see the heart of God. Likewise, when we know Jesus, we know the heart of the Father. John 3:16 says, "For God so loved the world, that He gave His only begotten Son, that whoever believes in Him should not perish, but have everlasting life." Everyone who is a Christian knows this verse by heart but may not have stopped to think deeply on this verse. Why did Jesus have to come? Because we were separated from God. How were we separated from God? Man's sin separated Him from God. How did God reconcile man to Himself? By the death of Jesus on the cross and the shedding of His blood. Why do we have to believe on Him? To have everlasting life, as believing on Him washes away our sins, which leads us to the heart of God. At His very heart is the demonstration of His love through forgiveness of our sins. And Jesus came to demonstrate the will of the Father regarding forgiveness of sins by laying down His own life to purchase our forgiveness. Sin created separation between us and God, as God is a holy, just, and righteous God; so He must punish sin. Through Jesus, God created a way for forgiveness of those sins, so we do not receive the punishment we deserve for those sins.

PARABLE OF THE UNFORGIVING SERVANT

Jesus demonstrates this great forgiveness by God and our need to forgive in the parable of the unforgiving servant. Background of the story is that there is a king who was owed by his servant "very much money"[5] who "could pay nothing he owed."[6] The king ordered that "he and his wife and his children and all that he had should be sold to pay what he owed."[7] The servant then begged to give him time so that he could pay all that he owed. "Then the king took pity on his servant and let him go. He told him he did not have to pay the money back."[8] The parable continues on in that this same servant who was forgiven of a large debt "went out and found one of the other servants who owed him very little money. He took hold of his neck and said, 'Pay me the money you owe me!'"[9] This man's servant of course begged for more time, so he could pay the debt, but he was not given time and thrown into prison. The master (the king) found out about this and called the servant whom he had forgiven the large debt and said, "'You bad servant! I forgave you. I said that you would not have to pay back any of the money you owed me because you asked me. Should you not have had pity on the other servant, even as I had pity on you?' The king was very angry. He handed him over to men who would beat and hurt him until he paid all the money he owed."[10] Most people want their debt removed by God, but then they do not forgive others of the debt against them. The parable ends with a stern warning from Jesus: "So will My Father in heaven do to you, if each one of you does not forgive his brother from his heart."[11]

The concept of money was used to get across the point of forgiveness. Most people understand money and debt, and those terms are used for people to grasp the importance of what took place here. Say you have a credit card on which you owe one million dollars and you do not have a job to pay it off, but the credit card company miraculously wipes out this amount of debt without any cost to you! And you have a friend who owes you one hundred dollars and has not paid; so you stop talking to him and take him to court in order to get him to pay. This is the point of the parable! The beauty of this parable points to what God did through Christ; He wiped away a debt we could not pay on the cross and wants us to do the same in return to those who do wrong to us.

Jesus demonstrated the will of the Father not only through one of His last statements on the cross when He said, "Forgive them for they know not what they do,"[12] but also throughout His time here on earth. Jesus walked the earth, seeking and saving those who were lost. He was always ready to forgive those who repented and turned to Him, and never once in the Bible will you find Him saying, "I don't forgive you." It must be mentioned that there is a sin not forgiven of men, and that is blasphemy of the Holy Spirit.[13] The Pharisees, on the other hand, were unforgiving and supposedly the righteous ones at that time. They got mad at Jesus for forgiving people of their sins. Jesus warned us that our righteousness needed to "surpasses *that* of the scribes and Pharisees."[14] Jesus had quite a few showdowns, so to speak, with these Pharisees. One showdown occurred in (John 8:1-10), when a woman was taken in the very act of adultery and was going to be stoned. Jesus intervened on her behalf, just as He did for everyone on the cross, and forgave her of her sins. However, they had every right by the Law to stone her, but Jesus did not condemn her. An important part of that story is that He made a statement to the Pharisees and the crowd: "He who is without sin among you, let him be the first to throw a stone at her."[15] Of course, the story goes that each one, from the oldest to the youngest, left as they all realized they had sinned as well. Maybe this lesson should be for us too when we start to hold things against other people and want them to pay for their sins. We might ask ourselves this question: Are we without sin? And do we have the right to cast stones? No, we are not without sin, and we do not have the right to cast stones. In fact, Jesus said, "Whenever you stand praying, forgive, if you have anything against anyone."[16] That is *any*, meaning anyone no matter what he or she did. Yes, it can be painful, but God gives us the grace to do it. Also, Jesus realized our humanness, and that we could be easily offended. That is why He said to forgive "whenever" we pray. We need to pray and forgive on a daily basis as we can be offended on a daily basis.

HARDNESS OF HEART

We have discussed that our unforgivingness means that our "Father who is in heaven"[17] will not then forgive us of our sins. However, unforgivingness can also impact us in our emotions (depression and anxiety) as well as in our physical bodies. One of the other most important effects is that it leads to is hardness of heart. With a hard heart we will not experience peace or joy, we will not receive what God wants for us from His Word, and we will not produce fruit in our lives.

The devil wants to destroy the ripe soil, which is our hearts, before the Word of God can be planted in it. He does this because he realizes that if the Word of God is planted in good soil, it will produce fruit. Therefore, if he can get us to harden our hearts, he can then steal any fruit that may be produced from it, and God desires us to "bear much fruit."[18] In addition, we are the keepers of our heart, and it is our responsibility to make sure our heart is right. Proverbs says "Watch over your heart with all diligence, for from it *flow* the springs of life."[19]

Hardness of heart leads us into bondage. Hardness of heart led Jonah into the belly of a "great fish", and yes, Jonah was unforgiving. The story is not just about Jonah and the "great fish." Within the story is imbedded the true meaning of the story that Jonah had a hard heart that was unforgiving, and that God is merciful to all. Jonah's hardness of heart was against the Ninevites because of their history with Israel. Israel was God's chosen people, and he was one of them. As we have established, Jonah did not want Nineveh to receive repentance and forgiveness.[20] Unfortunately, it took him three days and three nights in the belly of the "great fish."[21] Only then did he get out of the belly of the whale and go to Nineveh. He preached in Nineveh, and they all humbled themselves, from the king to the least, and God had mercy on them.[22] After the Ninevites were saved, Jonah wanted to die. He had such resentment against the Ninevites that even though He obeyed God in going in Nineveh, he still was bound by unforgivingness.[23] In fact, Jonah asked God to "take"[24] his life from him as he would be better off dead than alive. God asked Jonah, "Do you have good reason to be so angry?"[25] Jonah actually thought he had a right to go to death being angry. God had mercy on him in his disobedience, but Jonah was angry that God forgave Nineveh and actually had no right to be mad.

Does this sound like you, disobeying God by not forgiving others as God has done with us? We often choose not to forgive, as we do not feel they deserve it, just like Jonah thought that forgiveness was not right and that he was justified in being angry at Nineveh. Sometimes the other person has hurt us so badly that we do not feel like forgiveness is appropriate. We begin to become wise in our own eyes, forgetting we are disobeying God and clouding our vision. Unforgivingness leads to bitterness, grudges, hatred, judgment, strife, and resentment. We may even have thoughts (like Jonah) that the person who offended us should not receive forgiveness and be saved. We may want that person to go to hell or pay for what he or she has done to us. That was not God's will for Nineveh, and it is certainly not His will for the people of today. In fact, we may pray to God to punish those people who have hurt us and make them pay, and not hold on to the fact that vengeance is the Lord's as the Bible says, "O LORD, God of vengeance"[26] This is what Jonah did after God had such great mercy on the "exceedingly great city" because of the fact that it had "more than one hundred and twenty thousand persons" in it "and much livestock."[27] Jonah 4:5 says, "So Jonah went out of the city and sat on the east side of the city. There he made himself a shelter and sat under it in the shade, till he might see what would become of the city."[28] Essentially, Jonah was standing in judgment against them because of their status as sinners and because they were not the chosen ones like those of Israel. God does not need us to be the judge, as there is only one Judge. Nor does He need us to do His job by attempting to punish others. But He does require us to forgive. From the book of Jonah, it is clear that God is the only one who decides on the punishment or pardoning of a person's sins.

RELATIONSHIPS AND FORGIVENESS

There is a section of this book that deals with relationships and the importance of having relationships with people and God. However, these interesting institutions called "relationships" provide an opportunity for pain as well. In fact, we participate in relationships from birth, and unfortunately, none of us have choices in which family we are born into. It is out of these relationships that our biggest pains, disappointments, tragedies, abuses, mistakes, hurts, wounds, and brokenness can come. These relationships create a foundation for further hurts and pains in our lives, which keep us in bondage to our painful past and continue to perpetuate ongoing emotional baggage that we carry from one relationship to the next.

I am aware that people do some pretty rotten things to other people. These could be mentally, sexually, and emotionally. In my clinical practice, I have heard some heartbreaking stories about experiences that my clients had endured. One man had endured long-term abuse that was unjustified and undeserved. This man had held a grudge for so long that this man began experiencing digestive problems and his hair started falling out. These problems had developed only after holding the grudge for a long time. This man thought that he was going to make his abuser pay for what he had done to him, but he ended up paying himself with physical problems. I have heard it best said—"unforgivingness is like drinking poison and expecting the other person to die." Relationships may be the biggest source of our pain, but forgivingness provides the biggest and best opportunity for healing, deliverance, and putting the past to rest so it does not impact our current lives.

FEELINGS AND FORGIVENESS

When we forgive someone, we cannot determine whether or not we really have forgiven them based on our feelings. A patient in my "Old Emotional Baggage" group explained forgiveness. He said, "Forgiveness is a choice in you giving it over to God, saying that you are leaving it in His hands and that you will not hold what that person did against you." I thought that this was pretty good. So forgiveness is a choice on our part and one that is a part of our life as a Christian. We must be able take the offense against us and measure it against the multitude of wrongs for which God has forgiven us and easily forgive. My friend Garr is a wonderful example of forgiveness. He realizes the great amount of wrong that was forgiven him by His Father in heaven and quickly lets anything go that happens between him and his wife.

Feelings are a barrier in the process of forgiveness because we may still experience anger toward that person and interpret that anger as unforgivingness. We cannot live by our feelings; we need to live by the truth. We need to make the decision to forgive those who have wronged us. We can even be angry with someone, but we are to "not let the sun go down on our wrath." We are told to "be angry and do not sin." We can be angry without sinning. Anger becomes a sin when we continue to hold on to it for long periods of time. In looking at "do not let the sun go down on your wrath," we probably need to make sure that we have made a choice to forgive in our evening prayers as to "not let the sun go down on your anger"[29] or the day ending in unforgiveness.

We cannot overlook that the hurt needs to be healed in this forgiveness process as well. Forgiveness is not saying what someone did to us was deserved, right, or warranted. So what about those feelings we have that jump up within us if that person is in the room with us and we have forgiven them? For one, let us not beat ourselves up about these feelings, but realize that we are human and as a human being have been hurt by another person. Most likely, feelings are arising out of the fact that someone has indeed done us wrong. We need God to heal the wounds in order to mend them. Therefore, we make a choice to forgive and then ask God to heal whatever wound was caused. We cannot continue to hold on to anger or other feelings that may arise from a person's wrongs.

BLESS THOSE WHO CURSE YOU

Forgiveness is the first part of the action as God holds us to a higher standard. The next step is to bless the person that hurt or offended you. The Bible says to "bless those who curse you, pray for those who mistreat you."[30] This may bring up indignation in people, and they may say, "Oh no, I think I can forgive, but bless them . . . No way!" or, "They don't deserve it; you know what they did to me?!" Well, think about the cross. Did we deserve the forgiveness? No, but God chose to forgive us anyway, and He did so while we were His enemies. God so richly blessed us through Jesus Christ and He wants us to bless others as well, even those who hurt us and whom we consider enemies. He wants us to have this same heart in praying for blessings upon those who have hurt us. We may not want to pray or bless or forgive them; however, Jesus says, "But I say to you who hear, love your enemies, do good to those who hate you, bless those who curse you, pray for those who mistreat you."[31] Blessing those who hurt us begins a change in our hearts and identifies us with the merciful heart of God. It gets us out of the bitterness, and we then begin to walk in that mercy. As we walk in mercy, we become Christ's ambassadors as well. We shine Christ's light, and we become imitators of what Christ has done upon the cross . . . forgive.

Unforgivingness is a trap. We can be God-fearing just as Jonah and say we are Christians but not walk out forgiveness as God wants us to. In this regard, we become merely hearers of the Word and not doers of the Word. Unforgivingness is not only a trap but also a doorway for the enemy to come in because it allows him access to our lives. The Lord knows your every thought at every given moment, and He sees your actions. What about your thoughts? Are they honoring to God or not? Are you walking out the Word of God in this area of forgiveness? Or are you holding on to unforgivingness that results in depression?

Extreme Examples of Forgiveness

Forgiveness is often easier to talk about than to actually do. It is easy to struggle with the area of forgiveness, and I think that it is not something that comes natural to a person and something we can only do by God's grace. I can give accounts of my struggles with simple situations of forgiveness, such as when my wife says something to me that I do not like and hold on to it for a little while. And there are many times I know that I need to forgive but actually choose not to, because I do not feel like it at that moment. Fortunately, in the end, God reminds me of the need to forgive and I try and walk in forgiveness.

There are many stories I have heard while working in the mental health field which I cannot comprehend. I have heard stories about parents prostituting their five-year-old-child for drugs, about parents prostituting their teenage daughter for drugs, about men raping little girls, about sexual abuse by parents, and about abuse by spouses. I can somehow disconnect from these stories in that something of this degree has never happened to me, but I can recognize the struggle someone has with the concept of the command by God to forgive others. Of course, there are many feelings and beliefs that these kinds of people do not deserve forgiveness at all. These people have every right to be mad and no reason to really forgive.

These aforementioned examples are difficult, and it really blows my mind when someone forgives in these extreme situations. There are many examples of victims of childhood sexual abuse forgiving the abuser, of parents of murdered children forgiving the murderer, of victims of rape forgiving the rapist, and so forth. The parable of the unforgiving servant is an extreme example by the master who was owed the great debt. I am reading through the book *Jesus Freaks* again, which is a book about Christian martyrs. These Christians, in spite of suffering unspeakable acts of violence, not only forgave but also continued to love their abusers and pray for them as they were dying, being raped or having their children killed in front of them. I read these stories and wonder if I would have the same reaction toward these people if I were in that same condition. But somehow forgiveness is possible even in the most extreme situations. I am not sure if they refuse to be labeled a victim, is it that they love Jesus so much that they forgive, or is it that they realize how much they have been forgiven and know that they did not deserve forgiveness either? It is interesting to ponder this concept of forgiveness and begin to apply it in our lives and see freedom begin to take place from the bondage of the past. It would be great to lose the chains from the past which has directly impacted the ability to move forward, no longer being a slave to the emotions, beliefs, or behaviors associated with that slavery.

CHAPTER SEVEN

HOPELESSNESS

HOPE IS SOMETHING THAT EVEN the mental health field has identified as playing an important role in a person's recovery. Many people with depression suffer from hopelessness. They are overwhelmed living with depression on a daily basis and might see their future as unbearable if continuing to live this way. It is difficult for them to find hope in anything, and they cannot see the hope that others may have for them. Many of my patients have put their hope in other people which ended up disappointing them. The pitfall of having your hope wrapped up in other people is that people will fail you. People are fallible and will make mistakes. For my friend who committed suicide, it was a combination of putting his identity in his job and putting his hope in a relationship, and he perceived that both were ending. He was in his early sixties and thought that if his relationship and job ended, he would not be able to find anyone else or a different job. He thought he would be all alone and his situation was hopeless. The Bible tells us not to put our trust in people. Psalm 118:8-9 it says, "It is better to trust in the Lord than to put confidence in man, it is better to trust in the Lord than to put confidence in princes."[1] Psalm 146:3-4 says it this way: "Do not put your trust in princes, nor in the son of man, in whom there is not help. His spirit departs, he returns to his earth; in that very day his plans perish."[2]

People also put their hope in money. This issue has come to the forefront in times of financial crises. The current national financial crisis has resulted in a sudden loss of wealth and an increase in suicide. From the article "Do suicides go up when the economy heads south?": "In light of these recent deaths, many people are wondering: Do suicide rates spike when the economy is in trouble? Yes, say experts. 'We ordinarily experience much, much higher rates of suicide during times of recession,' says M. Harvey Brenner, professor of public health at the University of North Texas Health Science Center and Johns Hopkins University in Baltimore, Maryland."[3] People have put all their hope in something that can be taken away in a matter of minutes. The Bible warns the rich about this problem in 1 Timothy 6:17: "Command those who are rich in this present world not to be arrogant nor to put their hope in wealth, which is so uncertain, but to put their hope in God, who richly provides us with everything for our enjoyment."[4]

Christians are called to find hope in the Lord and also put their hope in Him. He is the only one in whom all hope is really found. There is hope in nothing else in this life, and there is only one who can bring hope into our lives. There is hope for each one of us in the Lord if we put our trust in Him. We need to rely on Him and go to His Word in order to see what He has to say about hope, because in God and in His Word "surely there is a future and your hope will not be cut off."[5] God is a "hiding place and my shield,"[6] "our help and our shield,"[7] rest for our souls, our truth and guide, and our "unfailing love."[8]

There is hope that God will be with a Christian in the midst of his or her depression. There is also hope that God will heal the Christian. But there is also the greatest hope of all—the hope of salvation and the resurrection of the dead. Hope is essential. Without hope, a person is destined to live a life of emptiness. Proverbs 13:12: "Hope deferred makes the heart sick, but a longing fulfilled is a tree of life."[9] Psalm 27:13 reads, "I would have lost heart, unless I had believed That I would see the goodness of the Lord In the land of living."[10]

Without hope a person can easily stay in the bondage and oppression of depression. We need to be like Abraham, as expressed in Romans 4:18; he had hope "against all hope" in what God had told him about his life and future. The chapter and verse do not really give the full account of what was going on with Abraham, but his story is outlined in Genesis. In short, Abraham was promised offspring, but his wife was barren and he was beyond childbearing age. The great thing about him is that he kept hope in spite of all the obstacles and barriers against him. He could have given up and given in to what his age was telling him and what his wife's circumstances were telling him, but he remained hopeful that God was going to do what He said He would do. Many years later, God delivered on the promise of a child by his wife when he and his wife were beyond child-bearing age.

This Bible account should give us hope in whatever situation we may find ourselves. God can do anything and "nothing will be impossible with God."[11] It does not matter if you have been depressed your whole life, it does not matter if you have been in a psychiatric hospital, it does not matter what diagnoses you carry, and it does not matter what the doctors say about you and your illness. It matters what God says about your situation.

THE VALLEY OF DRY BONES

There is a great song written by Michael and Lisa Gungor called "Dry Bones." A few of my favorite verses from this song are "These bones cry out, These dry bones cry for you To live and move 'Cause only You can raise the dead, Can lift my head up" and "Jesus, You're the one who saves us, Constantly creates us into something new, Jesus, surely you will finds us, Surely our Messiah will make all things new, Will make all things new."[12] These are great verses and speak to people who feel and believe that they are just a used-up, good-for-nothing, and dead-on-the-inside person. This song speaks directly to many people who are depressed and hopeless and see no purpose in their lives.

Israel experienced a time of greatness during the righteous King Josiah's reign. He cleansed Israel of false gods and their priests, repaired the temple, and restored reading from the book of the law. However, he was killed, and evil kings ruled in his place. Eventually, a king named Jehoiachin ruled, but he and many others, including Ezekiel the prophet, were deported to Babylon. Judah remained independent with King Zedekiah, but he rebelled against Nebuchadnezzar and Babylon. Zedekiah, his sons, and a lot of his army were put to death, and the people who were left were taken away captive to Babylon where Ezekiel was. The temple of God in Jerusalem was then burned. The people of Israel went from living the good life in the times of the reforms under King Josiah to captivity, destruction, death, and bondage. They were completely discouraged to the point that they said "Our bones are dry, our hope is lost, and we ourselves are cut off!"[13] They were hopeless.

But Ezekiel the prophet had a visit from God, who by the Spirit of God put him in the midst of this valley filled with dry, dead, and lifeless bones. God said something interesting to Ezekiel; he said, "Son of man, can these bones live?"[14] God goes on further to tell him to "Prophesy to these bones, and say to them, 'O dry bones, hear the word of the Lord! Thus says the Lord God to these bones: "Surely I will cause breath to enter into you, and you shall live.""[15] Ezekiel listens to God and "prophesied," and as he "prophesied, there was a noise, and suddenly a rattling; and the bones came together, bone to bone. Indeed, as I looked, the sinews and the flesh came upon them, and the skin covered them over; but there was no breath in them"[16] Ezekiel realized that there was "no breath in them." God then says, "Prophesy to the breath, prophesy, son of man, and say to the breath, 'Thus says the Lord God: "Come from the four winds, O breath, and breathe on these slain, that they may live.""" Ezekiel does, "and breath came into them, and they lived, and stood upon their feet, an exceedingly great army."[17] This "breath" he caused to enter them was the Spirit of God. In 37:14 God says, "I will put My Spirit in you, and you shall live."[18]

The work of a new life is a creative work of the Holy Spirit, as He is the one who recreates life in us. When we believe in God, He sends the Spirit of Jesus Christ into our hearts that recreates us in Christ. If we are Christians, it is the Spirit of God who started our regeneration process and renews us and recreates us. It is the very Spirit of God that breathes life into us! So let God's Spirit breathe life back into your hopeless situation. You might feel like your life is cut off and you are nothing but a dry and useless corpse, but God proves that He is powerful and can bring life in the valley of a person's despair, loneliness, and depression.

Chapter Eight

We Have an Enemy

THERE ARE PEOPLE WHO DO not realize that they have an enemy to their faith. If people are ignorant to this, it can lead to many defeats. Most people actually believe that there is a devil, but they are deceived into thinking that he is not affecting people once they get saved. Others may think that the devil does not exist, which is also deception. We do have an enemy, and he will attempt to deceive and destroy us. Revelation points out the devil's tactics. It says, "And he cast him [devil] into the bottomless pit, and shut him up, and set a seal on him, so that he should deceive the nations no more till the thousand years were finished. But after these things he must be released for a little while."[1]

We do not need to have knowledge of the devil to give him glory in any way, but to realize we have an enemy that "prowls around like a roaring lion, seeking someone to devour."[2] The person he wants to devour is the Christian. We need to be aware that the devil is bold, as he deceived man into falling in the Garden of Eden and tempted Jesus in the wilderness. The devil tries to go up against God and Jesus, and he will be bold enough to attack us. And his intentions are to "steal and kill and destroy"[3] us in any way he can.

Christians are made for a specific purpose and plan by God. He has saved us to show his great works in us, and we are to shine the light of Christ into this world. He has given each of us a part to play in His body, which is the church. If the enemy can get us depressed or make our depression worse, he has achieved his mission of stealing and destroying the works we do in Christ's name. By doing so, he tries to bring the power of Christ and the image of his person to shame in order to try and discredit our faith and others' faith in him.

Those with depression may say that they do not have some great plan or purpose from God, but we must not forget that we all have a part to play in his body. We must also remember that to be greatest of all is to be a servant. That is what Christ desires. He does not care if it is vacuuming the church on Saturdays, picking up the trash, dusting, or watching children in the nursery. People with depression have low motivation and energy and do not want to participate in anything. And in not doing anything, the devil triumphs over the Christian (who is supposed to have dominion over the devil) and steals the works they could be doing in the name of Jesus.

We as Christians can make a large impact on other people's lives by serving them in the church through various ways. In fact, God has set "helps" ministry in the church, so all can and could participate in being the hands and the feet of the body of Christ. In 1 Corinthians 12:28, God says, "And God has appointed these in the church: first apostles, second prophets, third teachers, after that miracles, then gifts of healings, helps, administrations, varieties of tongues."[4] You may have missed it, but in that Scripture, "helps" ministry was listed. You may think that you cannot do it, but Philippians 4:13 says, "I can do all things through Christ who strengthens me."[5] Further, Moses was giving the children of Israel encouragement before they went to fight against several nations. He said, "Be strong and courageous, do not be afraid or tremble at them, for the Lord your God is the one who goes with you. He will not fail you or forsake you."[6] So start to take back the ministry, witness, and testimony you have through the "helps" ministry, and Christ will see it and reward you. Revelation 2:19 states, "I know your works, love, service, faith, and your patience; and as for your works, the last are more than the first."[7] Jesus knows our works, and in the aforementioned Scripture, He talks about our faith as well. The Bible talks about our faith and how we show our faith by our works as it is our faith in action. We are not saved by our works, but we do bring forth "works" when we have faith. "Faith Without Works Is Dead."[8] What does it profit, my brethren, if someone says he has faith but does not have works? Can faith save him? . . . But someone will say, 'You have faith, and I have works.' Show me your faith without your works, and I will show you my faith by my works."[9] You can bring glory to God by doing works and play your part in the body of Christ by following the command "Let your light so shine before men, that they may see your good works and glorify your Father in heaven."[10]

You may not think you are doing much by sweeping, vacuuming, shaking hands, being an usher, cleaning toilets, watching little kids in the nursery, or changing diapers, but you are, and you are playing your part for the kingdom. This is because Jesus calls the people who give food to the hungry, clothes to the naked, and water to the thirsty; those who visit the sick; those who take strangers into their home; and those who visit people in prison his sheep.[11] Interestingly enough, the people who do not do these things will go to the "eternal fire which has been prepared for the devil and his angels."[12] By doing these works, you really are showing forth Jesus into the world, and this will lead people to salvation. If you serve in the church, watching someone's children, and they get saved in the service, then you have played a part in this as well. Daniel 12:3 says, "Those who are wise shall shine Like the brightness of the firmament, And those who turn many to righteousness, Like the stars forever and ever."[13]

Another trick of the devil is to oppress people. In Greek, the word "oppress" means to "exercise dominion" over something (Strong's Concordance). When people are depressed, it feels like they have no control over it and succumb to depression's power. Many people do not feel like they have the strength or energy to fight it, and it seems like an insurmountable task to take on. Therefore, most people give in to this oppressive force called depression. What they are really telling me is that their depression is controlling or "exercising dominion" over their very life.

Someone may look at this and not believe that depression has anything to do with oppression or work of the enemy. But the devil will use your circumstances for his own desire. Further, if he does not cause the depression, he will manipulate it to make your life miserable. One of the definitions of "oppression" from the dictionary is "depression." This is right in line with what depression is, oppressive in nature. We need to have an accurate view of the devil and demons assigned to oppress people as well as oppression. Ephesians 6:12 says, "For we do not wrestle against flesh and blood, but against principalities, against powers, against the rulers of the darkness of this age, against spiritual hosts of wickedness in heavenly places."[14] Further, Ephesians 6:11 says,

"Put on the whole armor of God, that you may be able to stand against the wiles of the devil."[15]

We do not need to get overly focused on the fact the devil oppresses people. We need to focus on what we can do in order to be free from this oppressive spirit that invades people's lives. This comes from God's Word, and it is of course Jesus who will set us free. This is best said in Acts 10:38: "How God anointed Jesus of Nazareth with the Holy Spirit and with power, who went about doing good and healing all who were oppressed by the devil, for God was with Him."[16] This Scripture is important because it not only tells us that people are oppressed (depressed) by the devil but, more importantly, that Jesus went about "healing all" who were oppressed by him. We need to also be aware that Jesus showed His authority (dominion) over the devil and was victorious over him. This was displayed in Colossians 2:15, where it is talking about Jesus and says, "Having disarmed principalities and powers, He (Jesus) made a public spectacle of them, triumphing over them in it."[17] If you are not convinced about Jesus' authority over the enemy and his servants, then read Colossians 2:9-10: "For in Him (Jesus) dwells all the fullness of the Godhead bodily; and you are complete in Him, who is the head of all principality and power."[18] Essentially, you are safe in Christ and have His authority over all evil power.

Another deception of the enemy is to bring people into our lives that give us bad counsel or someone who causes us to stumble. The devil knows that with bad counsel our lives will unravel or continue to unravel. Bad counsel is just like having no counsel at all. Proverbs 15:22 says; "Without counsel, plans go awry, But in the multitude of counselors they are established."[19] Further, Proverbs 11:14 says, "Where there is no counsel, the people fall; But in the multitude of counselors there is safety."[20] We must be aware that we must make sure that the counsel we receive is godly counsel.

Let us not forget that we have an enemy who wants to "steal, kill, and destroy" us, and let us work diligently to not give him any foothold into our lives. In spite of our circumstances, God wants us to be servants and play our part in the body of Christ, so He has given us "helps" ministry to do this. God sees the small and the great things done in the body of Christ, so start to mix your faith that you have in Jesus Christ with "good works" for the kingdom of God. Also, let us seek out wise counsel that is of the Lord, so we can have prosperous ways in our lives.

One of the best ways to seek out counsel is to go directly to the Word of God itself. In it you will find all you need.

ERROR OF USING ALCOHOL/DRUGS TO COPE

As we have previously explained, when it comes to depression, there are many resulting feelings, emotions, thoughts, and even physical pains that are associated with it. These can lead a person to try anything he or she can to help alleviate them.

In particular, alcohol or illegal drugs use is a common method people may use to treat symptoms of depression. We will focus mainly on alcohol (beer, wine, hard liquor) in this section, but we are really implying any psychoactive substance (legal or illegal). We focus on alcohol, as we find that "alcohol, the most widely used psychoactive drug in the United States, has unique pharmacological effects on the person drinking it"[21] Alcohol may be the most commonly used substance because it is readily available. Alcohol use is a socially acceptable form of behavior in our society and within our churches. It is cheap to purchase and can have a positive impact on symptoms of depression. The difficulty with alcohol is that it has a positive impact on symptoms only for a short period of time. Alcohol does not fully take away depression symptoms, and a person has to continue drinking to treat symptoms that remain. A person could likely form an addiction to alcohol with many resulting negative consequences. There may also be a direct link between alcohol use and the formation of depression symptoms. Most detrimental is the fact that a person will likely experience deterioration in his or her relationship with God.

With the aforementioned in mind, we need to keep in mind what the Bible says about our use of alcohol and its negative benefits as well as its strong caution against the use of alcohol. We must also realize that we want to treat and be delivered from depression rather than making decisions that keep us entrenched in depression or making things worse with the depression from the negatives of alcohol use.

The following study, completed in 1998 by the US Department of Justice, sheds light on the significant problems created by alcohol use, abuse, and addiction. This report is extensive, so I have added only portions of this report to accentuate the information.

Some findings from the report:

- Among violent crimes the offender is far more likely to have been drinking than under the influence of other drugs, with the exception of robberies where other drugs are as almost as likely to have been used as alcohol.
- Alcohol is typically found in the offender, victim, or both in about half of all homicides and serious assaults, as well as in a high percentage of sex-related crimes, robberies, and incidents of domestic violence; and alcohol-related problems are disproportionately found among both juvenile and adult criminal offenders.
- Although there are fewer deaths from alcohol-related causes than from cancer or heart disease, alcohol-related deaths tend to occur at much younger ages.
- Alcohol can harm virtually every organ and system in the body.
- Alcohol is the single most important cause of illness and death from liver disease (alcoholic hepatitis and cirrhosis).
- Alcohol is associated with cardiovascular diseases such as cardiomyopathy, hypertension, arrhythmias, and stroke.
- Alcohol contributes to approximately sixty-five percent of all cases of pancreatitis.
- Alcohol depresses the immune system and results in a predisposition to infectious diseases, including respiratory infections, pneumonia, and tuberculosis.
- Alcohol increases the risk for cancer, with an estimated two to four percent of all cancer cases thought to be caused either directly or indirectly by alcohol. The strongest link between alcohol and cancer involves cancers of the upper digestive tract, including the esophagus, the mouth, the pharynx, and the larynx. Less consistent data link alcohol consumption and cancers of the liver, breast, and colon.
- Thirty-eight percent of all traffic fatalities (the leading cause of accidental death) are alcohol-related. Alcoholics are nearly five times more likely than others to die in motor vehicle crashes.
- Alcohol contributes to one hundred thousand deaths annually, making it the third leading cause of preventable mortality in the US, after tobacco and diet/activity patterns.[22]

An article titled "Alcohol Kills More Than AIDS, TB or Violence" found the following evidence:

- Alcohol causes nearly four percent of deaths worldwide, more than AIDS, tuberculosis, or violence.
- Approximately 2.5 million people die each year from alcohol-related causes,
- The harmful use of alcohol is especially fatal for younger age groups, and alcohol is the world's leading risk factor for death among males aged fifteen to fifty-nine.
- Alcohol is a causal factor in sixty types of diseases and injuries, according to WHO's first report on alcohol since 2004.
- Alcohol consumption has been linked to cirrhosis of the liver, epilepsy, poisonings, road traffic accidents, violence, and several types of cancer, including cancers of the colorectum, breast, larynx, and liver.[23]

THE BIBLE ON DRINKING ALCOHOL

Drinking and drunkenness are major problems in our society, and this problem is not any different in the body of Christ. The amount of Christians that drink and most likely get drunk is probably the same as that of non-Christians. This might be because some churches do not preach against it, because some churches accept it as a common practice as long as it is in moderation, or because churches or people find Scriptures that allow them to drink. Whichever the reason, drunkenness or even the use of substances need attention in the body of Christ, as God says, "My people are destroyed for lack of knowledge." [24] And there are many people in the church that are being destroyed by alcohol.

In light of all the negative consequences of drinking, there are many Christians who debate the topic. But within the church body itself, it remains a sensitive subject. The Bible speaks out strongly against being drunk. It also does not speak favorably about liquor, wine, or strong drink.

THE BIBLE ON DRINKING AND OTHER DANGERS

There are churches who preach on what the Bible says about alcohol. If they do, they might not go into depth of why it is so dangerous. Some might even preach on it from the standpoint that you may drink as long as it is in moderation. The Bible says, "Or do you not know that the unrighteous will not inherit the kingdom of God? Do not be deceived; neither fornicators, nor idolaters, nor adulterers, nor effeminate, nor homosexuals, nor thieves, nor the covetous, nor drunkards, nor revilers, nor swindlers, will inherit the kingdom of God."[25] Most importantly, in the destructive workings of alcohol is the fact that a person will not inherit the kingdom of heaven.

However, we must point out the other problems highlighted in the Bible. Working in a psychiatric hospital has really invaded my world with these destructive forces. I have worked with people who have killed their family member while driving drunk, have killed their friend while driving drunk, have lost businesses, have destroyed marriages, have lost homes, have lost all their material possessions, have committed crimes, and have abused spouses and children. Some other cases were where addicts engaged in prostitution, prostituted out their children, and have committed bestiality to continue to support their habits. I remember one young woman who was admitted to our inpatient facility on two separate occasions. She had become depressed, was in danger of losing her children, and had then begun to prostitute herself for drugs. The first I saw her, she looked pretty healthy and very attractive; she was still taking care of her body, hair, nails, and so forth. It was dramatic when I saw her about a year and a half later and saw the destructive force of the substances. This once attractive and young lady was almost unrecognizable to me. She looked much older than she was. She was emaciated and missing teeth. She had her children taken away from her, her marriage was over, and she was homeless. She had been severely beaten prior to coming inpatient over drugs. Remarkably, she was still not ready to give up the substances. These drugs had that much control over her and had completely destroyed her life. The terrible thing was that this young girl had grown up in church and was now separated from God and was not going to inherit the kingdom of heaven.

Unfortunately, I have worked with hundreds of patients in very similar circumstances. They cannot let go of the substances, even though they have cost them everything. Little do they know that they are fulfilling poignant Scriptures in Proverbs 23 which speak directly on addiction. The troubles and pain a person experiences are a direct result of using too much of a substance. Proverbs 23:29-30 says it this way: "Who has trouble? Who has pain? Who fights? Who complains? Who has unnecessary bruises? Who has bloodshot eyes? It is people who drink too much wine, who try out all different kinds of strong drinks."[26] When people start using substances, they do not think that they will be enslaved to them. They think that they are just out having a good time and enjoying time with friends. They do not realize that, even though their use of substances is enjoyable, "later it bites like a snake with poison in its fangs."[27] Eventually, their alcohol shows no mercy on them and turns deadly. And they continue to give alcohol control over their lives and fulfill the addict's statement "They hit me, but I'm not hurt. They beat me up, but I don't remember it. I wish I could wake up. Then I would get another drink."[28] At all costs, they continue to seek their alcohol, and addicts, no matter the substance, continue to seek their substance no matter the gravity of their consequences.

CHAPTER NINE

WELCOME TO THE JUNGLE

THIS TITLE, "WELCOME TO THE Jungle," is poignant in addressing this world as we know it and how many of us have experienced it. Sometimes it seems as if this world is a jungle and that people are no different than the animals. It seems, at times, that man is void of compassion and, even though man has the ability to reason, he does not use it and hurts others. There is one sure promise in this life: we will suffer persecution, trials, and tribulations. Even Jesus said that there would be persecutions in this life. This phenomenon does not make sense, but it plays out in our daily lives. King Solomon points out this phenomenon when he said, "Bad things happen to good people, and good things happen to bad people."[1]

Christians will suffer wrongs in this life. I am not trying to trivialize people's hurts, as Christians have suffered many wrongs and hurts in this. But we do need to remember that, "beautiful people experience undeserved hurt."[2] Unfortunately, this could lead to us asking why God is doing this to us, essentially blaming God. God gives us free will, so we can make any choice we want in this life. People are supposed to have the rule over sin, but there is much evil and wrongs that happen in this world that are not from God. Therefore, correct blame needs to be put on people who hurt others as well as the spirit behind these actions. We need to remember, "For we do not wrestle against flesh and blood, but against principalities, against powers, against the rulers of the darkness of this age, against spiritual hosts of wickedness in the heavenly places."[3] One thing for sure is that we will all suffer some types of hurts or pains in this life. Once again, Christians are not exempt from hurt and are susceptible to hurts and pains brought on by others in their lives.

Paul

Paul is one of those people in the Bible who experienced multiple hurts. Paul is an amazing figure in the Bible, as he is someone whom God had grace upon for murdering Christians and then used mightily for spreading of the gospel. Paul also wrote at least half of the New Testament. Even in the midst of God using Paul for mighty works and Paul's many victories, Paul suffered many persecutions. One of the primary persecutions that Paul faced was what the Bible calls a "thorn in the flesh."[4] This is something for which Paul sought the Lord to heal but never received relief from it. We cannot know what exactly Paul's "thorn in the flesh" was; it could mean sickness, temptation, persecution, or opposition. Taking a look at the Bible, it could be deduced that Paul had some type of physical illness, and that physical illness could have been a problem with his eyes. In the following Scripture, Paul talked about having a physical infirmity and then made a curious statement at the end of the set of Scriptures about people plucking out their eyes to give to him: "You know that it was because of a bodily illness that I preached the gospel to you the first time; and that which was a trial to you in my bodily condition you did not despise or loathe, but you received me as an angel of God, as Christ Jesus *Himself.* Where then is that sense of blessing you had? For I bear you witness that, if possible, you would have plucked out your eyes and given them to me."[5] Whether or not it was Paul's eyes, the Bible is clear that it has something to do with Paul's flesh which people could see per Paul writing "and my trial which was in my flesh you did not despise or reject, but you received me as an angel of God, even as Christ Jesus." Apparently, it was something people could see and likely reject him for it.

The importance of the aforementioned accounts of Paul's "thorn in the flesh" is to not focus on the infirmity itself or argue about what the specific infirmity was, but the fact that Paul continues to fulfill his calling in spite of it. This physically infirmity did not slow Paul down in his ongoing mission to "press on toward the goal for the prize of the upward call of God in Christ Jesus."[6] Also the true testament was to the people's faith to still receive Paul and what he had to say despite the infirmity. Maybe it was like Jesus' physical appearance where "there is no beauty that we should desire him,"[7] so people believed and followed Him not for His looks, physique, status, money, and so forth. They received and followed Him out of faith, received their healings by faith, and glorified God through Him.

Another testament to Paul was that he was always praising God, even in the midst of his affliction. Paul never glorified any sickness or disease, but continued to go about his work and did not even let being shipwrecked, bitten by a snake, imprisonment, rejection, or anything get in his way of the ministry and walk with God. Was it not Paul who penned, "And we know that God causes all things to work together for good to those who love God, to those who are called according to *His* purpose."?[8] Paul took "pleasure in infirmities, in reproaches, in needs, in persecutions, in distresses, for Christ's sake."[9] Paul wrote in 1 Thessalonians 5:17, "Rejoice always, pray without ceasing, in everything give thanks; for this is the will of God in Christ Jesus for you." It was all about Jesus for Paul.

JOB

There are people within the church that point to a person's sin as the reason they are afflicted with sickness and disease. We cannot forget the destruction of sin in our lives. Sin can allow the devil to attack us, as it opens a door to invite the enemy into our lives or, biblically speaking, gives him a "foothold."[10] But this narrow-minded thinking cannot account for why some people who are wicked and evil do not experience sickness and disease or why some Christians might experience sickness or disease or hardship in their lives. Job is one of those people from the Bible. The book of Job influences many people's thoughts about God, sin, and punishment.

Job is very blessed and has great riches and many children. He is famous for his knowledge, and people come to him in order to receive his godly wisdom. People are blessed by his advice. For some reason, God allows Satan to afflict Job. Job's ten children die, he loses all of his wealth, and his whole body is afflicted with boils. Job becomes distressed, down, and depressed. He states, "the LORD gave and the LORD has taken away. Blessed be the name of the LORD."[11] and "through all this Job did not sin nor did he blame God."[12] Some people believe that Job sinned by saying that God did bad and good or that he gave and took away, but the scriptures clear it up by stating that Job did not sin after making these statements.

His wife comes to him and tells him to curse God and die. His own wife is now against him. However, he does not curse God and says that they should accept "good" from God's hand as well as "bad." And even "in all this Job did not sin with his lips."[13] Once again, he does not sin in saying that "good" and "bad" come from God's hands.

His three friends then come to him and are in silence as they do not know what to say as Job is in such poor condition. However, when they do speak, they accuse Job of sin, as their view is that God only punishes those who have done wrong. They berate him because he does not repent, and they get judgmental and condemning.

Job never curses God, but he reasserts his righteousness and demands from God to know what he has done to deserve this punishment. He also curses the day he was born and wished for the grave. Many individuals come in to see me at the hospital who do not actively try to die, but wish they would die in their sleep so they do not have to face the misery.

God eventually talks directly to Job and corrects him for the darkened counsel.[14] God never gives Job a reason for why he was afflicted, which is an interesting point from Job we need to take into consideration as it speaks to the sovereignty of God. God once again blessed Job and his family "consoled him and comforted him for all the adversities that the LORD had brought on him."[15] Further in Job it reads that the Lord restored Job's losses when he prayed for his friends. In fact, the Lord gave Job twice as much as he had before. "After this, Job lived 140 years, and saw his sons and his grandsons, four generations. And Job died, an old man and full of days."[16] It is important to note that God did not bless Job in the end because he had to, but because he is a loving, compassionate, and benevolent God.

THE END OF JOB

It has always been peculiar to me how pastors preach on Job. The curious part to me is that every pastor I have heard teach on it always had a reason why Job suffered the way he did. I find this curious because through all of Job's seeking for an answer, when God shows up he never gives Job an answer of why, but God responds with interesting statements and questions to Job. Pastors try and answer the question of why Job suffered because he must have done something! They get caught up, just like a person who is depressed, in the mess of the middle instead of the blessing of the end which is a main point of this story. There are many people who get caught up into the trappings of all that Job suffered, and they forget the end state of Job's life. They question more why would God do this rather than see that God is longsuffering and merciful. The Bible says, "Indeed we count them blessed who endure. You have heard of the perseverance of Job and seen the end intended by the Lord—that the Lord is very compassionate and merciful."[17] The purposes of talking about Job is that we need to realize that there could still be Jobs in this present day and that sickness or diseases (adversity) can still be allowed by God regardless whether or not a person is in sin. But the message is to "persevere" and to see the end of Job, which is the blessed life intended by God.

JOSEPH

Joseph was loved by his father more than his eleven brothers. He had two dreams that he would rule over his brothers. Unfortunately, he was open with his dreams and told his brothers, and their disposition turned toward Joseph. Further, Joseph's "brothers saw that their father loved him more than all his brothers; and so they hated him and could not speak to him on friendly terms."[18] We find out some time later that his brothers wanted to kill him; but God spared Joseph's life, and instead he was sold into captivity as a slave in Egypt. In spite of his slavery, "the Lord was with him"[19] and everything he did prospered and Joseph was a successful.

However, Joseph was wrongly accused by his master's wife of attempted rape and was placed in prison, but he had God's mercy in the midst of his circumstance and once again was successful and prospered in prison. There were two of the king's servants, a butler and a baker, who were placed in prison with Joseph, and he interpreted their dreams. The butler was eventually restored to serving the king and did not keep the promise that he would remember Joseph when he was restored to the king's service. Eventually, this butler remembered

Joseph's interpretation of his dream and recommended him to the king. Joseph was able to interpret a dream for the king of Egypt (Pharaoh) and was appointed "over all the land of Egypt."[20] Joseph's interpretation of the dream was that there was going to be a seven-year famine to hit the land, and he had a plan to where people would be able to eat during that time. We find that during the famine, Joseph's brothers had to come for grain in Egypt, the family was finally restored, and Joseph's dream he had had when he was seventeen was fulfilled as his brothers bowed to him.

GOD'S GREATER PURPOSE FOR JOSEPH'S SLAVERY

Joseph's life had a strange turn of events, and I am sure that he could not have predicted he would be plotted against by his brothers, sold into slavery, brought into a land of where he was afflicted, accused of rape, put in prison, forgotten, and then finally restored. I am sure that he did not know there would be almost two decades between his dream and the fulfillment of that dream when he was seventeen. A mistake could be that we read this story and be mad at his brothers and what they did, without realizing that Joseph's position over Egypt allowed for him to save many lives from starvation. It is interesting that Joseph was not mad at his brothers when they were finally restored to him and even told them to not be "angry or grieved" with themselves for what they had done to him, because it was God's plan all along:

Now do not be grieved or angry with yourselves, because you sold me here, for God sent me before you to preserve life. For the famine has been in the land these two years, and there are still five years in which there will be neither plowing nor harvesting. God sent me before you to preserve for you a remnant in the earth, and to keep you alive by a great deliverance. Now, therefore, it was not you who sent me here, but God; and He has made me a father to Pharaoh and lord of all his household and ruler over all the land of Egypt.[21]

Joseph's life took a dramatic turn of events, but it was God's plan and will all along. Joseph just continued to endure and then fulfilled God's purpose for his life.

KING DAVID

In the Bible, David is one example of someone who experienced depression a time or two in his life. And if you read the account of his life, you might think, *It sure makes sense that he was down at times.* We must look at the Scripture and see if David's condition of feeling down lasted a long time or if this condition was an ongoing battle throughout his life. We must also look at the Scripture to determine if there was a specific cause for his feelings of being down or where he was a weighed down in his emotions. In many psalms, David writes that God's hand was heavy on him for iniquity or his sins. In other psalms, David is down because of his enemies around him. Yet in other psalms, David writes that he is down because of those who were his friends but then turned on him.

In terms of depression, David does write in the psalms about his "soul being downcast." "Soul" is a person's mind, will, and emotions. "Downcast," according to the American Heritage Dictionary, could mean "low in spirits; depressed." David writes, "I am weary with my sighing; Every night I make my bed swim, I dissolve my couch with my tears. My eye has wasted away with grief; It has become old because of all my adversaries."[22] So it does appear that David experienced his periods of time when he was depressed.

David, like Paul, is another great example of someone who despite much adversity and many persecutions, continued to rely on God for strength and fulfilled his duties as God's appointment as king over Israel. In spite of his times of depression or down mood, David still experienced joy, still experienced peace, still walked in blessing and abundance, spent time in God's house, worshipped, and gave thanks to God. Also, David still performed his duties as a king, fought in battles, overthrew kings and nations surrounding Israel, and overcame giants.

There are interesting accounts in the Scriptures where David writes about his depressed state followed by his attitude toward it. "Why are you down in the dumps, dear soul? Why are you crying the blues? Fix my eyes on God—soon I'll be praising again. He puts a smile on my face. He's my God."[23] Also, "Return to your rest O my soul, for the LORD has dealt bountifully with you. For you have rescued my soul from death, my eyes from tears, my feet from stumbling."[24] In the aforementioned Scripture, David did not dwell on his state of emotions but spoke about his soul (mind, will, and emotions) and about God's deliverance and love for him. Unfortunately, most people who are depressed get caught up in the emotions rather than speaking and focusing on God's love for them and His deliverance that is available to them.

David's life was filled with many trials and tribulations on this earth. He faced a mocking giant and did not have the support of his brothers, he was sought for many years by King Saul to be killed, he was forced to live in caves, he lost an infant son and another son tried to take the throne from him, and much more. David was not perfect. He was an adulterer and murderer. However, he was a man after God's own heart. David lived a life that is memorable, as he always stayed close to God, repented for his sin, and had a pattern where he reminded himself of who his Lord was despite his circumstances.

DAVID ENCOURAGED HIMSELF IN THE LORD

One of the greatest things about David is the way he encouraged himself with God's Word. He shows a pattern of encouraging himself in the Lord. This ability to encourage oneself is difficult for many people who are struggling in the midst of their trials. Sometimes people are their own worst enemies and do not encourage themselves, but focus on the negatives. But we need to encourage ourselves by the words we speak, and these words should be from God's Word.

One of the greatest examples of David encouraging himself is after the Amalekites attacked the town (Ziklag), while David and his men were gone. They not only attacked this town but burned it with fire, "and they took captive the women *and all* who were in it, both small and great, without killing anyone, and carried *them* off and went their way."[25] David's own wives had been taken captive. David and his men returned to the city of Ziklag, saw what happened, and "lifted their voices and wept until there was no strength in them to weep."[26] What followed the weeping was disturbing, and David became stressed because of it. The "people spoke of stoning him," but "David strengthened himself in the Lord his God."[27]

David encouraged himself in the Lord while all those around him wanted to kill him. He encouraged himself through the Lord despite what his circumstances were. If people withhold their mouth from encouraging themselves, it might result in feeling more sorrowful about their circumstances, like in Psalm 39: "I was mute and silent, I refrained *even* from good, And my sorrow grew worse."[28] So we need to encourage ourselves with the words of our mouth that are, in fact, in line with God's Word. God's Word says, "A man has joy by the answer of his mouth, And a word spoken in due season, how good it is!"[29] and, "Pleasant words are like a honeycomb, Sweetness to the soul and health to the bones."[30] Just like Joseph, David persevered and endured all of his trials and afflictions and never walked away from God despite how bad it had become at times.

ELIJAH

Elijah is a great prophet of the Old Testament. He knew all too well, just like all the prophets and apostles of the Bible, the highs and lows of his walk with God. God worked many miracles by his hand. One of his most well-known miracles was that he prayed that it would not rain and it did not for three and a half years. It did not rain until Elijah prayed again that it would rain.

Another one of his miracles took place in the midst of the three and a half years it was not raining. This was a high moment in Elijah's life. Elijah was zealous for God, and he did not like the worship of gods who were not gods. He called the "450 prophets of Baal and 400 prophets of the Asherah, who eat at Jezebel's table"[31] to a place called Mount Carmel. There he posed a challenge to these men. Elijah said,

I alone am left a prophet of the Lord, but Baal's prophets are 450 men. Now let them give us two oxen; and let them choose one ox for themselves and cut it up, and place it on the wood, but put no fire under it; and I will prepare the other ox and lay it on the wood, and I will not put a fire under it. Then you call on the name of your god, and I will call on the name of the Lord, and the God who answers by fire, He is God.[32]

Of course the prophets of Baal accepted this challenge. They did as Elijah requested with the sacrifice and then called upon their god, but there was no answer. They then went to great lengths and "cried with a loud voice and cut themselves according to their custom with swords and lances until the blood gushed out on them."[33] Of course there was still no response from their god Baal, and Elijah mocked. Then it was Elijah's turn. He not only built an altar and cut up an ox but also dug trenches around the altar and poured water on it. "The water flowed around the altar and he also filled the trench with water."[34] Finally, Elijah prayed and "then the fire of the LORD fell and consumed the burnt offering and the wood and the stones and the dust, and licked up the water that was in the trench. When all the people saw it, they fell on their faces; and they said, 'The Lord, He is God; the Lord, He is God.'"[35]

It is interesting that following these great miracles that God did by Elijah's prayers and Elijah's hand, Elijah was on the run after a threat from King Ahab's wife Jezebel. 1 Kings 19:1-2 reads, "Now Ahab told Jezebel all that Elijah had done, and how he had killed all the prophets with the sword. Then Jezebel sent a messenger to Elijah, saying, 'So may the gods do to me and even more, if I do not make your life as the life of one of them by tomorrow about this time.'" It is interesting that Elijah was feeling so low and like a failure that "he requested for himself that he might die, and said, 'It is enough; now, O Lord, take my life, for I am not better than my fathers.'"[36] Many people who are depressed wish that God would take their life or that they would die somehow. Following this comment, Elijah became focused on the negatives of the situation instead of the positives and decided to go hang out in a cave. Two times the Lord came to Elijah and asked why he was hanging out in a cave, and Elijah replied twice, "I have been very zealous for the Lord, the God of hosts; for the sons of Israel have forsaken your covenant, torn down your altars and killed Your prophets with the sword. And I alone am left; and they seek my life, to take it away."[37] God's response was something less than what he probably hoped to hear in the midst of his poor circumstances. God replied with "Go, return on thy way to the wilderness of Damascus: and when thou comest, anoint Hazael to be king over Syria: And Jehu the son of Nimshi shalt thou anoint to be king over Israel: and Elisha the son of Shaphat of Abelmeholah shalt thou anoint to be prophet in thy room."[38] Elijah obeyed and did as God told him. Elijah obeyed even in the midst of his feelings of despair. God did not want Elijah sitting there and feeling sorry for himself.

HOLD FAST TO THE LORD (ENDURE)

These aforementioned testimonies, of prominent figures of the Bible, focus on them not as special people, but on that they are man just like we are. They went through these persecutions and trials as human beings. They made mistakes, got down and depressed, and even prayed for death. James 5:17 says about Elijah, "Elijah was a man with a nature like ours, and he prayed earnestly that it would not rain; and it did not rain on the land for three years and six months." David, Elijah, Paul, and Job were men with the same nature we have. The only reason why we hear about their great trials and tribulations is the way they handled them: they held fast to God and they endured. Paul wrote to the Thessalonians, "Therefore, we ourselves speak proudly of you among the churches of God for your perseverance and faith in the midst of all your persecutions and afflictions which you endure."[39] There is importance of endurance in our walk with God and in the midst of life's trials. But the true beauty is what that endurance will produce in the end.

A STORY OF PRESENT-DAY ENDURANCE

My sister Kristie is a great hero of faith for me as well as a picture of endurance and perseverance during extremely difficult times. I remember receiving the call from my mom that fateful morning telling me through sobs that my nephew had died during the nighttime. It was my sister Kristie who found him that morning, still warm, but lifeless and not breathing. My brother in law's attempts to revive with CPR went in vain. The forty-minute drive from my house to the hospital seemed like an eternity, one I could not drive myself because of my own emotional and mental state. We all sat in the private room at the hospital, not knowing what to say. The only sound was the sobbing of those present there. It was surreal. Even in my anguish, I could not even imagine to begin to touch what was going on emotionally and mentally with my sister and brother-in-law. I cannot capture their emotion; so my sister graciously put the experience in her own words:

> Derrin, even as I write this, sometimes I think everything
> is still so raw that I think I haven't really dealt with

everything the way I should. Sometimes when we're strong, I think we just barrel through everything without really dealing with the matter or embracing the grief and dealing with it, but I know that in these things I write below—I have found peace so many times with God, and He is the way, He is the healer, and I'm still a work in progress.

Everyone deals with grief in their own way. For me, I remember the first two weeks I spent each morning literally lying on the floor on my face in prayer. So many people want to question God, but I was too scared to. I know everything happens for a reason and that He was the One who could help. Knowing that my son was in heaven, safe in the arms of Jesus is really where I found my solace and strength. He is in much better hands than mine. I would have to remind myself of that daily. An incident that happened as a reminder of where my son was and how mindful God is of me goes like this— about two or three weeks after Braxton passed away, we were headed home from the gym (Paul, Colton, and me). It was about a 20 minute ride, but nobody said anything on the way. We were all lost in our own world and our own thoughts. Mine, of course, were about Braxton. We pulled into the driveway in silence, and I was still lost in my thoughts when Paul said "Did you hear that?" "What," I asked. Colton, then 2 years old, had just said "It's ok, Braxton's with Jesus." It brought me to tears. God had used my 2 year old son to bring me comfort in that moment. He affirmed through him that my son truly was in heaven with Him. That was a moment I'll never forget. God loves us so much, and He wanted me to know right then that I could find comfort in Him. Despite that, I obviously had ups and downs. I had days where I had moments that I have labeled as "freight train days" because I would be working or doing whatever, and the grief would suddenly hit me—like a freight train. There were times at work that I would have to go into the bathroom because I knew that tears could spill over any second, and I didn't want to embarrass myself. There are some things you just don't want to talk to people about because it hurts so much, and unless someone has lost a child, they really don't understand. It just felt kind of useless to talk to many people about my emotions—I didn't want my family to be more burdened for me than what they already were, I didn't think anyone would understand or truly KNOW what I was going through, I didn't feel they could help anyway even if they understood, and most of all, I knew God was the only one who could help. Every day, I just had to remind myself that Braxton was in heaven. That, having a 2 year old to take care of, and the hopes of having another child kept me going through that time. I heard a speaker on Focus on the Family speaking about how he had lost his wife, and someone had said to him "embrace the grief." He said he had no idea at the time what they meant, but I knew what it meant. Just like him, I probably wouldn't have understood it in the beginning either, but I see it now. Embrace the grief—it's there, deal with it, don't push it aside, and don't just try to take your mind off it. Face it, embrace it, and let God do the healing that He wants to do. I am still healing to this day. Some days it still feels raw when I think about it, but it's nothing like it was in the beginning. I don't believe anyone completely overcomes a loved one's death. I believe we are constantly a work in progress in the healing department. I knew I had to choose to pick myself up and carry on and not let my entire life be defeated by this grief.

So, the key thing that got me through this was knowing that Braxton was in heaven. That he would never feel pain, sorrow, or grief and that someday I will see him again, and it will be as if we never missed a day.

Kristie battled anxiety and depression during the following weeks and lost eight pounds within the first week after Braxton's death. She would experience heavy bouts of extreme feelings of heaviness (depression) which would relent only with prayer. She still struggles to this day, but her story is one of enduring. She still has a relationship with God, never walked away from Him, and continues to serve Him to this day. This, to me, is an extreme example of enduring no matter the circumstances and being an over-comer through Jesus Christ.

CHAPTER TEN

PRAISE: BECAUSE HE IS GOD

FIRST AND MOST IMPORTANTLY, OUR praise is to God because of who He is. Praise is not to get a feeling but to lavish Him with something for which He is due. Praise is defined as "to give an offering of grateful homage in words or songs, as an act of worship."[1] This could be a hymn we sing to God, dancing before Him. We do not praise God for a feeling, but it could be a secondary benefit from praising God. There are many people who praise Him only for the feeling, but that is not the reason we praise God. We praise Him because there is no one like Him[2]; He is holy and glorious and does great wonders[3]; He is the one and only great God, we are in great awe of Him[4]; He is "King of all the earth"[5]; and because "the Lord is good, his mercy is everlasting and his truth endureth to all generations."[6]

PRAISE . . . IT'S OUR ENTRY INTO THE PRESENCE OF GOD

Psalm 100:4 says, "Enter his gates with thanksgiving, and his courts with praise. Give thanks to him, bless his name."[7] Praise is our entrance into the presence of God, and we need to "come before His presence with singing" as outlined in the aforementioned Scripture. Have you ever noticed that the first thing we do when we come to church is having a praise and worship service? This praise and worship service sets the tone of the whole service. It is the entrance into the presence of the Lord. Praise uplifts our spirit because it is focused on God. Getting together in one accord and one purpose magnifies the name of Jesus. Jesus promises to be in the midst of us as we are gathered together in His name. As we begin to praise and worship our God, His is with us.

And wonderful things can happen when we come into the presence of the Lord and get focused on Him.

For each individual, it could be that they start their day with praise, worship, and thanksgiving to God. It is solely by God's grace and loving-kindness that we are even given each day. If we can enter into each day with praise, it will set the tone of our whole day. Even the Word says, "This is the day which the Lord has made; let us rejoice and be glad in it."[8]

Praise for God's Grace and Mercy

Another reason to praise God is for the grace He has shown on us. It is by God's grace and loving-kindness that we have been led to repentance and that our souls have been saved from hell. His grace is really "favor,"[9] which is something God gives us that we have not earned. Ephesians 1:5-7 demonstrates this grace of God through Christ and shows how much we have to be thankful for and to praise Him in this world: "He predestined us to adoption as sons through Jesus Christ to Himself, according to the kind intention of His will, to the praise of the glory of His grace, which He freely bestowed on us in the Beloved. In Him we have redemption through His blood, the forgiveness of our trespasses, according to the riches of His grace."

Praise Gives Victory over Enemies

In the Bible there are two stories of Jehoshaphat in which he sought the Lord's will before going into battle. In 2 Chronicles 20, Jehoshaphat used praise and God destroyed his enemies. Jehoshaphat was fearful when he found out that a great multitude of enemies were coming "to make war against"[10] Judah and Jerusalem. However, Jehoshaphat fixed himself and his mind to "seek the Lord, and proclaimed a fast throughout all Judah."[11] He then brought all the people together and prayed. God responded, "Do not fear or be dismayed because of this great multitude, for the battle is not yours but God's."[12] Then "Jehoshaphat bowed his head with his face to the ground, and all Judah and the inhabitants of Jerusalem fell down before the Lord, worshiping the Lord. The Levites, from the sons of the Kohathites and of the sons of the Korahites, stood up to praise the Lord God of Israel, with a very loud voice."[13]

On the day of the battle, Jehoshaphat encouraged the people in the Lord by saying, "Listen to me, O Judah and inhabitants of Jerusalem, put your trust in the Lord your God and you will be established. Put your trust in His prophets and succeed."[14] Jehoshaphat then followed this up with something amazing: "He appointed those who sang to the Lord and those who praised *Him* in holy attire, as they went out before the army."[15] As the people were singing and praising, "the Lord set ambushes against the sons of Ammon, Moab and Mount Seir, who had come against Judah; so they were routed"[16] or defeated. Jehoshaphat and all the people of Judah and Jerusalem returned to Jerusalem "with harps, lyres and trumpets to the house of the Lord"[17] and praised God for giving them victory over their enemies.

Jehoshaphat had the choir out front of the troops praising the Lord. Praising the Lord brought them the victory. It required their trust in the Lord. When Jehoshaphat first heard of the army coming toward them, he sought the Lord. He did not act out of his feelings but sought and trusted the Lord. He fasted, got others in agreement with him, and gave God praise. He gave God thanks for the victory. Depression says, "isolate yourself; life is not great; don't you feel heavy? stay in bed; God does not love you; you're a nobody; others don't understand you; God's not going to bring you through this" and so forth." But when you get up and praise God, you send confusion to the devil. It is the opposite of what he wants you to do. The devil is into pity parties. They are the kind of parties he likes to show up at. Praise is not a pity party. It is the exact opposite. The devil shows up, thinking this will be a great party and saying, "Let's see how low she/he can get today"; but when the praise music begins and you throw up your hands toward heaven, he wants to leave. The devil does not like to stay in places where someone is praising God.

PRAISE BREAKS CHAINS

Let us take a look at the account of Paul and Silas. They were sitting in jail, cold, tired, bound with chains, and bleeding from having been beaten with rods. But "at midnight Paul and Silas were praying and singing hymns to God, and the prisoners were listening to them.

Suddenly there was a great earthquake, so that the foundations of the prison were shaken, and immediately all the doors were opened and everyone's chains were loosed."[18] Their circumstances were not pleasant and could have stolen their motivation to praise, but they did not let it. They made the choice to praise God in the midst of the mess they had going on. "The thief comes only to steal, and kill and destroy,"[19] but Paul and Silas did not let him. The devil tries to steal your motivation and drive to praise God. He kills your ability to feel pleasure and enjoy activities. He plants thoughts of suicide in your mind to destroy you. He is a killjoy in every sense of the word. He gets you bound in the chains of heaviness in order to stop you from praising God. You have to take back the joy that was stolen, and although it is a struggle to praise God, the choice has to be made to put on the "garment of praise for the spirit of heaviness."[20]

PRAISE BRINGS DOWN THE WALLS

An amazing act of praise to God with voice and instruments was when the children of Israel overthrew Jericho. Joshua was leading the children of Israel and spoke to the Lord before this victory took place and God instructed him in what to do. Joshua 6:1-5 says,

> Now Jericho was tightly shut because of the sons of Israel; no one went out and no one came in. The Lord said to Joshua, "See, I have given Jericho into your hand, with its king and the valiant warriors. You shall march around the city, all the men of war circling the city once. You shall do so for six days. Also seven priests shall carry seven trumpets of rams' horns before the ark; then on the seventh day you shall march around the city seven times, and the priests shall blow the trumpets. It shall be that when they make a long blast with the ram's horn, and when you hear the sound of the trumpet, all the people shall shout with a great shout; and the wall of the city will fall down flat, and the people will go up every man straight ahead.

Just how the Lord said it would happen is how it happened. I would imagine Joshua and the Israelites did not understand why to praise the Lord at Jericho. Just imagine how Joshua may have felt telling the troops and the band the battle plan. Some of them may have thought it was silly. However, they were obedient and gained victory. Give the Lord a shout of praise! Praise gets the darkness out and exalts the Light. The light of Jesus Christ shines. Praise will get your mind off problems or feelings and onto the one who can knock down your walls of depression, your walls of regret, or the walls of your past.

PRAISE GOD FOR SALVATION

Another person known for being in bad situations is Paul. Look at Paul's life. He ran into many trials and suffered many persecutions, but he was always rejoicing. Paul himself penned "sorrowful, yet always rejoicing; poor, yet making many rich; having nothing, and yet possessing everything." [21] Paul found reasons to praise the Lord even in the bleakest of situations and in every situation he was in. One specific example is when he was arrested for no wrongdoing and sent to Rome to stand trial. He was on a ship to Rome in a terrible storm and sure to be shipwrecked. All of the others had lost hope in the midst of this situation. Some wanted to abandon the ship, and the guards were initially given orders to kill all the prisoners. However, in the midst of this chaos, Paul remembered a promise from God and stated, "Cheer up!"[22] because he believed it will be just as God said it would be! We as believers can also take this advice from Paul and "cheer up" in the midst of our circumstances; and we cannot get mad at Paul for saying this, because he took cheer and praised God in all of his fiery trials. If we still cannot find anything to give praise, we only need to look as far as the cross because Jesus suffered the affliction of the cross for us. We only need to look at the cross because Jesus laid down his life for us, so we did not have to shed our own blood. Habakkuk 3:17-19, which is "A Hymn of Faith," says, "Though the fig tree should not blossom, nor fruit be on the vines, the produce of the olive fail and the fields yield no food, the flock be cut off from the fold and there be no herd in the stalls, yet I will rejoice in the LORD; I will take joy in the God of my salvation. GOD, the Lord, is my strength; he makes my feet like the deer's; he makes me tread on my high places."[23] Essentially, you have more reasons to praise God than you do to keep silent. Habakkuk is making the point that even if you have no material possessions, wealth, or food, you can still "joy in the God of your salvation." Habakkuk realized that God is the God of his salvation, which is the most important thing.

Put on the Garment of Praise

Jesus came to give us "the oil of joy for mourning and the garment of praise for the spirit of heaviness."[24] "Heaviness" is an old word for "depression." Depression can be the enemy's tactic to get our minds on our problems and off how great God is, but praise helps us to magnify God instead of our situation. So "praise the name of God with a song And magnify Him with thanksgiving."[25] It is common for those struggling with depression not to feel like praising God. So at times it may be a sacrifice to give praise. In spite of the struggle for the depressed person to offer praise to God, Hebrews 13:15 says, to "continually offer the sacrifice of praise to God, that is, the fruit of our lips, giving thanks to His name." Even in the midst of his trial, Job states, "For I know that my Redeemer lives, and He shall stand at last on the earth."[26] It is important to put on the garment of praise that Jesus has given us. Play worship music, read the Psalms, make up your own songs, or make a list of what God has done for you and thank Him for it. Praise can break down the walls surrounding our heart and can give us the victory, like the Israelites at the walls of Jericho. Praise breaks the chains of hopelessness, lifts heaviness, and exalts God above any situation you may face. Isaiah 61:3 says to put on the "garment of praise for the spirit of heaviness."[27] The key is that you have to put it on. At times this may feel like a sacrifice. It is something you have to do. Most people with depression do not put this practice into action. Praise can be a powerful weapon for us against the enemy if we choose to "put" it on. Praise is not something we only utilize when we feel under attack, but we can use it at all times. God wants us to be victorious, and praise allows us to be victorious regardless of the situation.

King Saul's Example

There are many accounts of the purpose and power of praise in Scripture. However, no other set of Scriptures speak to the power of praise against demonic forces like 1 Samuel. King Saul had not followed an order given by God spoken through the prophet Samuel. As a result, God had rejected King Saul from no longer being king, and "the Spirit of the Lord departed from Saul."[28] After the Lord's Spirit departed from Saul, Saul began to experience an evil spirit that "terrorized him."[29] King Saul also consulted a seer, or what we would consider a medium or psychic. Saul's servants recognized that an evil spirit was "terrorizing" Saul and sought out a man who was a "skillful player on the harp"[30] in order that Saul would experience peace and be well. Saul's servants found David, who had God's anointing and who was a "skillful musician, a mighty man of valor, a warrior, one prudent in speech, and a handsome man."[31] Saul recognized the anointing David had on his life, and David found favor in King Saul's eyes. Saul requested that David play the harp when the evil spirit was troubling him, and "Saul would be refreshed and be well, and the evil spirit would depart from him."[32] Saul and his servant knew that praise would chase away the evil spirit, and Saul would then be well. Therefore, we can use this same method to chase away the enemy, just like Saul.

We see from the account in the Scriptures that there was refreshment for King Saul at the time that David played for him, but his heart was not right and the refreshment would leave when David was done praising God with his instrument. Saul was using David's anointing only to give himself relief without a true heart change. We need to praise and worship God for who He is, and not what we can get from Him, which shows a true heart of worship. When we come to God in true praise and worship, it shows that we are doing it out of a right heart. Also, we find that if we are like King Saul, we will need to get a "fix" from praise and worship all the time; but the underlying heart condition is still there. The most important information in this account of the Scripture is that we can use praise and worship in the same way David did. David drove away the evil spirit that was harassing Saul by worshipping and praising God.

CHAPTER ELEVEN
FOR THE CHURCH

PERCEPTION

B EING A CHRISTIAN HAS BEEN interesting, as I have encountered many people's perceptions of Christians, which influences their views of all Christians and God. People's perceptions of Christians range from crazy, to "Holy Roller," to hypocrite, to weak. These perceptions are not accurate, but frame a people's perceptions of Christians and eventually how they engage and participate in a relationship with Christians. Perception is an interesting concept for Christians as well because it guides their walk with God and ultimately how they treat others. However, perceptions can be skewed or inaccurate. And it is easy for Christians to be one-dimensional in their thinking, especially when it comes to God and how He views a disease such as depression.

EXAMPLES OF PERCEPTIONS

"I don't understand how a Christian can be depressed!" was the statement from the pastor behind the pulpit. I pondered this statement and realized that if a person has this perception, it immediately makes it difficult to connect with a person who is experiencing depression.

I remember a question and response in a class at church which is common throughout some parts of the body of Christ. The question was about the sickness of depression and where it came from, and the response was, "They got themselves a demon!" This one-dimensional thinking limits the person's ability to connect with a depressed person.

"There is something getting in the way of you being healed!" "Are you sure you don't have some hidden sin from you past?" This is an actual question I heard when a person was praying for me to be healed from a problem in my body. This perception was that I should be healed, but because of some moral deficit of mine, I was not experiencing God's healing.

"If that person was really a Christian, he wouldn't be the way he is!" This is a specific statement made by a coworker of mine who was a Christian. He was speaking about a patient in the psychiatric hospital who was depressed and anxious.

I had a chance to get to know a man from my church who was involved in the choir. He and his wife had been pregnant several times, and each one resulted in a miscarriage. Another member of the choir stated to him, "You just need more faith!"

These aforementioned statements or questions demonstrate a person's perception and can lead to a judgmental Christian and are ultimately pushing a person away from God. The most important thing we must avoid as Christians is making those who are Christians feel distant from God or make them walk away from God.

Beyond a Christian's perception problem is the problem of always settling on one cause behind a person's condition such as depression. This is what I call the Pharisee perspective. Unfortunately, many Christians fall within this "Pharisee perspective" when looking at sickness or any other condition of man, such as poverty. The disciples fell into this trap when questioning Jesus about a blind man's condition. John 9:1-3: "Now as Jesus passed by, He saw a man who was blind from birth. And His disciples asked Him, saying, 'Rabbi, who sinned, this man or his parents, that he was born blind?' Jesus answered, 'Neither this man nor his parents sinned, but that the works of God should be revealed in him."[1] What it does is bring the reason for a person's condition solely back to that person believed to be causing it somehow. This is what I believe was discussed in the book of Job when Job's friends were trying to provide causes for Job's condition, such as sin or pride.

Perceptions need to be accurate in terms of the causes for depression or any other sickness or disease. Correct perceptions for the cause of any illness needs to be prayerful and Holy Spirit-led. In looking at the Word of God, there are actually several explanations for the causes of sickness or disease. Anxiety can cause depression as stated in Proverbs 12:25:

"Anxiety in the heart of man causes depression, But a good word makes it glad."[2] Sin itself also has consequences. James 1:15 says, "Then when lust has conceived, it gives birth to sin; and when sin is accomplished, it brings forth death." Also, God will pour out His "fury"[3] on sin; "sin shall have great pain."[4] Jesus also talked about a connection between sin and sickness, disease or infirmity. Jesus healed a man who was sick with an "infirmity of thirty eight years."[5] Jesus warned this man about sin and said, "See, you have been made well. Sin no more, lest a worse thing come upon you."[6] Iniquities, which is defined as sin, is also an important concept to explore in the Bible and the resulting consequences of these iniquities.[7] There is a visitation of consequences of parents' iniquities on the generations that follow.[8] However, there might not be a connection between a person's sufferings and their parents' sin.[9] The devil can "oppress"[10] or afflict someone with an illness, such as "boils."[11] There can be a demonic[12] influence or "spirit of infirmity."[13] And we cannot leave out that man lives in a fallen state because of the sin Adam committed in the Garden of Eden and that we now live in a physical body that is susceptible to sickness and disease. From the moment of our birth, we are in the process of aging and moving toward our death; it is a process of decay. Other times our own decisions or life circumstances lead to depression. The key for Christians is not to get caught up in one perception of sickness or disease and have a balanced approach.

If We Are the Body . . . ?

We are living in a day and age where many people are consumed with themselves and their own needs. We do not seem to see much of the fulfilling of the scriptural command to love of others as we love ourselves. It seems that many people do not want to get involved in the life of a person who is suffering from depression and distance themselves from them. But for Christians, loving and serving those who are in need is an echo of the Bible as well as part of the greatest commandment in the Bible. Luke writes "And He said to him, 'What is written in the Law? How does it read to you?' And he answered, 'You shall love the Lord your God with all your heart, and with all your soul, and with all your strength, and with all your mind; and your neighbor as yourself.' And He said to him, 'You have answered correctly; do this and you will live.'"[14] This is what the Jesus deals with in addressing a lawyer's question about how to inherit eternal life. This lawyer was trying to catch Jesus in a mistake to accuse Him from the Law; and most people of today miss Jesus' answer, which is to love God with all of your being and then pour out that love by treating everyone with love. Let us take a closer look at what Jesus meant by loving "your neighbor as yourself" in His response to the lawyer.

The Good Samaritan

> Jesus replied and said, "A man was going down from Jerusalem to Jericho, and fell among robbers, and they stripped him and beat him, and went away leaving him half dead. And by chance a priest was going down on that road, and when he saw him, he passed by on the other side. Likewise a Levite also, when he came to the place and saw him, passed by on the other side. But a Samaritan, who was on a journey, came upon him; and when he saw him, he felt compassion, and came to him and bandaged up his wounds, pouring oil and wine on them; and he put him on his own beast, and brought him to an inn and took care of him. On the next day he took out two denarii and gave them to the innkeeper and said, 'Take care of him; and whatever more you spend, when I return I will repay you.' Which of these three do you think proved to be a neighbor to the man who fell into the robbers' hands?" And he said, "The one who showed mercy toward him." Then Jesus said to him, "Go and do the same."[15]

There could have been many reasons why the priest and the Levite did not help the "half dead" man. Some have expounded that the priest and the Levite were coming back from their time in the temple and would not have wanted to defile themselves, because if they became defiled, they would have had to offer an animal sacrifice, which would have cost them something. Or that they were worried about their own welfare, as the area was known for criminal activity. Or that they thought that this man was suffering because of his own sin. I believe that Jesus was taking a moment here to correct those who were supposed to know that law but yet were not living it out. The lawyer thought that he was righteous and was proud of himself that he knew the greatest commandment of the law, but he lacked putting the law into practice, and that is what Jesus was pointing out. We should not get too caught up in why the Samaritan helped the beaten man, but why the priest and the Levite did not help the man. This is essential for Christians, as we Christians are supposed to be the righteous ones of this time and day. This is what a Christian should take from this story: When we call ourselves Christians and say we love God, we also need to love others. Loving others shows that the love of God is in us and means getting involved in their lives in the midst of their mess. And their mess could mean their depression.

PRAY, PRAY, PRAY

Depression takes much energy and strength from the person who is suffering from it. The people who are involved in their lives might find it extremely difficult to find the right things to say to them. They also might think that the depressed person is not trying hard enough or even faking their depression. They might tell them to just "get over it"—that old "pull yourself up by your bootstraps" mentality. They might yell at the depressed person or get so frustrated that they withdraw completely from them. I remember, in the midst of my deep depression, my family would say they were concerned for me, but did not know what else to say and withdrew from doing anything. Most people do not know what to do or say to a depressed person. But the best anyone can do for a depressed person is pray, encourage them, and be supportive. This in no way voids the depressed person's responsibility to pray as the Bible says in the book of James, "Is anyone among you suffering? Then he must pray. Is anyone cheerful? He is to sing praises. Is anyone among you sick? Then he must call for the elders of the church and they are to pray over him, anointing him with oil in the name of the Lord."[16]

Unfortunately, many Christians are not praying for their suffering, nor are Christians praying for those who are in the chains of depression. And if we are praying, we might not pray diligently, daily, or fervently. It is sometimes easy to distance ourselves from the depressed person and the struggles they are having with depression, therefore not really going into continual prayer for their healing. Our prayers might be prayers that are short and lacking any true depth or substance. When we pray for one another it should be "without ceasing,"[17] in "night and day,"[18] "continuing steadfastly,"[19] and "always laboring fervently."[20] One might say that depressed Christians should be praying for themselves, but there is a burden on Christians to pray for one another. Even Jesus prayed for those who believed in Him: "I do not pray for these alone, but also for those who will believe in Me through their word."[21]

One great example from the Bible in regards to prayer offered up for another Christian was when Peter was placed in prison. "Peter was therefore kept in prison, but constant prayer was offered to God for him by the church."[22] As the church was constantly praying for Peter, "an angel of the Lord stood by him, and a light shone in the prison; and he struck Peter on the side and raised him up, saying, "Arise quickly!" And his chains fell off his hands."[23] The angel then led Peter "past the first and the second guard posts," and then through the final "iron gate"[24] which Peter exited to freedom. Peter said to himself "Now I know for certain that the Lord has sent His angel, and has delivered me from the hand of Herod and from all the expectation of the Jewish people."[25] There is power in our prayers for other Christians and our prayers do "accomplish much."[26]

ACCEPTANCE INTO THE CHURCH BODY

Depression takes a toll on a person's willingness to take active steps to participating in life, especially in the body of Christ. Maybe this is due to the nature of depression, which at times incapacitates an individual by attacking their confidence, making them feel shame, stealing their energy, and overwhelming them with heaviness, hopelessness, and worthlessness. However, it could be because many people, even if not depressed, believe they have to be perfect to step into a church or have to put on some type of fake act in order to fit in. It is just like being in a church that only thinks you are saved by the fact that you have no problems, have all the answers, say the right things, or dress and act a certain way. I remember a fellow Christian making statements about a patient at the psychiatric hospital with anxiety and depression. He implied if this person had in fact been a Christian, then he would not have been at a psychiatric facility. There are Christians who look more at the outside than what is going on inside a person. Thankfully, Jesus looks on a person's inward man and at the "circumcision" of the heart.[27] In fact, Jesus made a lot of comments about the Pharisees and how they made the outside (their clothes, looks, appearance) look great, "but inside they are full of dead men's bones and all uncleanness." [28] I grew up in a church that judged people like this, and I come across a lot of Christians in church today who think in these same terms.

This is a shortcoming in the church that inhibits a Christian's ability to work effectively with people who have problems. And the fact is the church is probably at the forefront of dealing with depression with the exception of the mental health field. There needs to be a show of acceptance on the Christian's part to deal effectively with Christians whose lives are being run by depression.

People with depression need to feel loved, accepted, and confident that they can go to the church and get the help they need. If the church cannot offer effective help, then it can lead the person to withdraw from the church and seek help somewhere else possibly with devastating results. Therefore, the church itself needs to cultivate an environment that is accepting of a person and one that reaches out to those in need, especially when they are in the depths of depression. Creating this kind of environment can foster relationships for people with depression and bring them into a larger community in which human relationships are necessary. We all are needed members in the body of Christ.

COMPASSION AND GRACE FOR OTHERS

Christians can be condemning of others and might not have mercy on those in the grips of depression. I have seen many Christians have more compassion toward sinners than Christians who are in the midst of a struggle. We too soon forget the forgiveness extended to us by Jesus Christ through His death and the instances when we were "ungodly."[29] We cannot forget all of the wonderful things that Christ has set us free from as well.

Christians are supposed to show forth the light of Christ. We cannot show this light if we are quick to judge those in the midst of despair and push them away from God. We need to receive those people and love them in order for them to receive that healing to their broken heart and not add more complications. After all, Jesus Christ came to "bind up the brokenhearted."[30]

Christians need to show compassion on those around them, no matter their situation, as God wishes that none "of these little ones should perish."[31] God rejoices in mercy, and it grieves Him deeply to have to punish someone. God finds no joy in punishing someone, but humans, who have been made in the "likeness of God,"[32] somehow find it joyous or justified when others suffer.

We see a lot of this grievance in our churches today, and we condemn people instead of praying for them and helping them through their situation of difficulty. We judge them as doing something wrong or living in sin. We think that because we practice things better or are not suffering from something like depression or anxiety, somehow God loves us more when that is not true at all. God loves us all the same; He said in Genesis that the pinnacle of His creation was man, and He saw that all He had created was "very good."[33] Instead of seeing with God's eyes and His heart of compassion, we see through fleshy eyes that do not have any compassion.

I learned something wonderful about true compassion from a psychiatrist where I worked. He had been a longtime Christian and was truly closer to the image of Christ than most. I hope to be more like him one day. I remember a specific case in which a man came into the psychiatric hospital who had molested his children and great-grandchildren. He knew what he had done was wrong, and he did not hide it from the treatment staff, but he was still having problems adjusting to the consequences of his actions. Further, this man had also been abused sexually when he was young as well. This psychiatrist had a lot of compassion on this man, although he did not say the man's actions should not have consequences. He thought the man needed counseling and forgiveness. I, of course, identified with the victims more and had compassion on them and really wanted the man to pay for what he had done to these people. I did not realize until later, when this psychiatrist died unexpectedly, what a true man of compassion he was. It is always easier to have compassion on the victims, but it takes a better person to have compassion on those we do not think are worthy of that compassion. This particular psychiatrist had compassion on both parties but, most importantly, on the man whom most would not have compassion on. This reminds me of the fact that we were in sin when Christ died for us, and we needed His compassion.

BROTHERLY LOVE

God wants us to love one another like He loved us when He gave us his best—Jesus! His love is based on the fact that Christ died for the all of mankind while we were still in sin and not based on what we do or have done. It is in His love that we are directed to love one another. However, we notice that within our churches, many hearts are closed up and do not follow the command to love one another.[34] And by not loving one another, they are not obeying a command that God has spoken in His Word. But when we do love, "His love is perfected in us"[35] and everybody will know that we are Jesus' disciples.[36]

Jesus had a lot to say about loving God and loving one another. Jesus dealt with a lot of religious leaders who were very judgmental and were not righteous in the least. They lacked love toward God in their hearts, and instead obeyed tradition (the Law) that could not make anyone perfect. Jesus talked about this issue of love with them, trying to move them from the letter of the Law to the law of love he established. In Matthew 22:36-40 Jesus says, when questioned by a lawyer about the greatest commandment in the Law, "Master, which is the greatest commandment in the law? Jesus said unto him, Thou shalt love the Lord thy God with all thy heart, and with all thy soul, and with all thy mind, this is the greatest commandment. And the second is like unto it, Thou shalt love thy neighbor as thyself. On these two commandments hang all the law and prophets."[37]

Most people do not have trouble with loving God, but have much difficulty with loving other people. Therefore, they are breaking the second part of this commandment set forth by Jesus Christ Himself. James 3:8-12 says it this way:

> But the tongue can no man tame, it is an unruly evil, full of deadly poison. Therewith bless we God, even the Father; and therewith curse we men which are made after the similitude of God. Out of the same mouth

proceedeth blessing and cursing. My brethren, these things ought not so to be. Doth a fountain send forth at the same place sweet water and bitter? Can the fig tree, my brethren, bear olive berries? either a vine, figs? so can no fountain both yield salt water and fresh.[38]

The conclusion is that God loved us and that we should love others as He commanded us. This means that we need to love those who are in the midst of depression and not judge them one way or the other. We can love them by not condemning them.

CONCLUSION

D EPRESSION IS A COMPLEX ILLNESS with various levels of intensity to the suffering person. Therefore, the old "pick yourself up by your bootstraps" mentality will not quite cut it. Nor will the "just get over it" attitude. Even though there is much known about depression, there is much more yet to be learned. And a specific cause cannot yet be pinpointed. Fortunately, there is help for those suffering from depression; but the treatments provided range in their effectiveness to fully treat depression, and a person could continue to suffer from remaining symptoms. There is also what is considered treatment-resistant depression that does not get better with the standard treatment of medications; more invasive treatment such as electroconvulsive therapy is then indicated.

When it comes to spiritual care, for those who are depressed, the mental health system and the churches of today are limited. A person can be left without a sense of hope from God in the midst of depression and some could move away from a relationship with God as well as be pushed away by well-meaning Christians. Hopefully, this book has allowed for people with depression not only to be encouraged but also to become reconnected and strengthened in their walk with God.

CITATIONS

INTRODUCTION

1. Revelation 1:8.
2. Matthew 1:23.

CHAPTER ONE

1. "Just Over Half of Americans Diagnosed with Major Depression Receive Care," National Institute of Mental Health, January 04, 2010, http://www.nimh.nih.gov/science-news/2010/just-over-half-of-americans-diagnosed-with-major-depression-receive-care.shtml.
2. Ronald C. Kessler et al., "Prevalence, severity, and co-morbidity of twelve-month DSM-IV disorders in the National Co-morbidity Survey Replication (NCS-R)," *Archives of General Psychiatry* 62, no. 6 (2005): 617-27.
3. "Depression: More Than a Chemical Imbalance," Carey A. Krause, Pine Rest Christian Mental Health Services, accessed March 20, 2012, http://66.241.236.120/resources/today/depression/depression.asp.
4. Paul E. Greenberg et al., "The Economic Burden of Depression in the United States: How Did It Change Between 1990 and 2000?," Journal of Clinical Psychiatry 64, no. 12 (2003): 1465-75.
5. Paul E. Greenberg et al., "Depression: a neglected major illness," Journal of Clinical Psychiatry 54, no. 11 (1993): 419-26.
6. American Psychiatric Association, *Diagnostic and Statistical Manual of Mental Disorders*, 4th ed. (Washington, DC: American Psychiatric Association, 1994).
7. "What Are the Signs and Symptoms of Depression?," National Institute of Mental Health, accessed February 12, 2012, http://

www.nimh.nih.gov/health/publications/depression/what-are-the-signs-and-symptoms-of-depression.shtml.

8. "Learning From History: Deinstitutionalization of People with Mental Illness As Precursor to Long-Term Care Reform," prepared by Chris Koyanagi, Kaiser Commission on Medicaid and Uninsured, August 2007, http://www.kff.org/medicaid/upload/7684.pdf.

9. The website for Abilify; Abilify.com.

10. The website for Seroquel XR; SeroquelXR.com; "Depression."

11. "Depression: More Than a Chemical Imbalance," Carey A. Krause, Pine Rest Christian Mental Health Services, accessed March 20, 2012, http://66.241.236.120/resources/today/depression/depression.asp.

12. "Dealing with Treatment-Resistant Depression: What to Do When Treatment Doesn't Seem to Work," Mental Health America, accessed March 21, 2012, http://www.nmha.org/index.cfm?objectid=C7DF95AB-1372-4D20-C85CA470535945CD.

13. "Placebo, Antidepressants May Lift Depression via Common Mechanism," National Institute of Mental Health, May 1, 2002, http://wwwapps.nimh.nih.gov/science-news/2002/placebo-antidepressant-may-lift-depression-via-common-mechanism.shtml.

14. "What Causes Depression," National Institute of Mental Health, Revised 2011, http://www.nimh.nih.gov/health/publications/depression/complete-index.shtml

15. "Longitudinal association of vitamin B-6, folate, and vitamin B-12 with depressive symptoms among older adults over time," prepared by Kimberly A. Skarupski; Christine Tangney; Hong Li; Bichun Ouyang; Denis A. Evans; and Martha Clare Morris, American Journal of Clinical Nutrition, May 2010, http://www.ajcn.org/content/92/2/330.full#ref-23.

16. Ibid.

17. "Depression and Dehydration," accessed February 11, 2012, http://www.waterbenefitshealth.com/depression-and-dehydration.html.

18. Ibid.

19. Ibid.

20. Proverbs 12:25 (ESV).

21. "Depression and Dehydration," accessed February 11, 2012, http://www.waterbenefitshealth.com/depression-and-dehydration.html.

22. Gordon Parker et al., "Omega-3 Fatty Acids and Mood Disorders," *American Journal of Psychiatry* 163 (2006): 969-78.

23. "Depression" Vitamin D Council, September 27, 2011, http://www.vitamindcouncil.org/health-conditions/mental-health-and-learning-disorders/depression/.

24. "The Obesity and Depression Link," Willow Lawson, *Psychology Today*, May 1, 2003, http://www.psychologytoday.com/articles/200305/the-obesity-depression-link.

25. "Hypothyroidism and Depression," WebMD, accessed March 21, 2012, http://www.webmd.com/depression/hypothyroidism-and-depression.

26. "Psychotherapies," National Institute of Mental Health, accessed March 20, 2012, http://www.nimh.nih.gov/health/topics/psychotherapies/index.shtml.

27. Ibid.

28. "Diagnostic Evaluation and Treatment," National Institute of Mental Health, accessed February 12, 2012, http://www.nimh.nih.gov/health/publications/men-and-depression/diagnostic-evaluation-and-treatment.shtml.

29. "Depression: More Than a Chemical Imbalance," Carey A. Krause, Pine Rest Christian Mental Health Services, accessed March 20, 2012, http://66.241.236.120/resources/today/depression/depression.asp.

30. "In Second Try to Treat Depression, Cognitive Therapy Generally As Effective As Medication," National Institute of Mental Health, accessed March 20, 2012, http://www.nimh.nih.gov/science-news/2007/in-second-try-to-treat-depression-cognitive-therapy-generally-as-effective-as-medication.shtml.

31. "Psychotherapies," National Institute of Mental Health, accessed March 20, 2012, http://www.nimh.nih.gov/health/topics/psychotherapies/index.shtml.

32. Dennis Greenberger and Christine A. Padesky, *Mind Over Mood: Change How You Feel by Changing the Way You Think* (New York: Guilford Press, 1995), v.

33. Ibid., 129.

34. Ibid., 129-130.

35. Ibid., 129.

36. "Psychotherapies," National Institute of Mental Health, accessed March 20, 2012, http://www.nimh.nih.gov/health/topics/psychotherapies/index.shtml.
37. Ibid.
38. Ibid.
39. Ibid.
40. "Brain Stimulation Therapies," National Institute of Mental Health, accessed March 20, 2012, http://www.nimh.nih.gov/health/topics/brain-stimulation-therapies/brain-stimulation-therapies.shtml#George.
41. "Diagnostic Evaluation and Treatment," National Institute of Mental Health, accessed February 12, 2012, http://www.nimh.nih.gov/health/publications/men-and-depression/diagnostic-evaluation-and-treatment.shtml.
42. "Brain Stimulation Therapies," National Institute of Mental Health, accessed March 20, 2012, http://www.nimh.nih.gov/health/topics/brain-stimulation-therapies/brain-stimulation-therapies.shtml#George.
43. Ibid.
44. Ibid.
45. Ibid.
46. "About Depression," TMS Center of Wisconsin, accessed March 20, 2012, http://tmscenterwisconsin.com/depression-tms/.
47. "Brain Stimulation Therapies," National Institute of Mental Health, accessed March 20, 2012, http://www.nimh.nih.gov/health/topics/brain-stimulation-therapies/brain-stimulation-therapies.shtml#George.
48. "Brain Stimulation Therapies," National Institute of Mental Health, accessed March 20, 2012, http://www.nimh.nih.gov/health/topics/brain-stimulation-therapies/brain-stimulation-therapies.shtml#George.
49. Ibid.
50. "Vagus Nerve Stimulation Successful for Depression," Doctor's Guide, accessed March 20, 2012, http://www.pslgroup.com/dg/15131a.htm.
51. "Brain Stimulation Therapies," National Institute of Mental Health, accessed March 20, 2012, http://www.nimh.nih.gov/health/

topics/brain-stimulation-therapies/brain-stimulation-therapies.
shtml#George.

52. Ibid.
53. Ibid.
54. Ibid.
55. 2 Timothy 3:16-17.

Chapter Two

1. "Depression: More Than a Chemical Imbalance," Carey A. Krause, Pine Rest Christian Mental Health Services, accessed March 20, 2012, http://66.241.236.120/resources/today/depression/depression. asp.
2. Ephesians 4:23.
3. John 8:44.
4. John 15:26; John 16:13.
5. 1 John 4:6.
6. Titus 1:2.
7. Jiaquan Xu, et al., "Deaths: Final Data for 2007," *National Vital Statistics Reports* 58, no. 19 (May 20, 2010): 5, table B, http://www. cdc.gov/nchs/data/nvsr/nvsr58/nvsr58_19.pdf.
8. Ibid.
9. Proverbs 18:9 (AB).
10. Colossians 4:14.
11. 2 Kings 20:7 (KJV).
12. Jeremiah 8:22.
13. Jeremiah 8:22 (NIV).
14. "Balm of Gilead," Wayne Blank, Church of God Daily Bible Study, accessed February 13, 2012, http://www.keyway.ca/ htm2003/20030221.htm.
15. Luke 10:34 (NKJV).
16. "Medicinal Uses of Olive Oil," Kulbhushaan Raghuvanshi, accessed February 15, 2012, http://www.buzzle.com/articles/medicinal-uses-of-olive-oil.html.
17. Ibid.
18. Luke 5:31 (emphasis in original).
19. Deuteronomy 18:10 (KJV).
20. Romans 1:17; Hebrews 10:38.

21. Exodus 15:26 (KJV).
22. Luke 8:43 (NKJV).
23. Luke 8:44 (NKJV).
24. Luke 8:46 (NKJV).
25. 2 Chronicles 16:11-12 (KJV).
26. Matthew 9:13; Matthew 12:7.
27. Matthew 9:36; Matthew 14:14; Matthew 20:34; Mark 1:41.
28. Mark 1:40-42 (NKJV).
29. Colossians 2:9 (AKJV).
30. Hebrews 13:8 (NKJV).
31. John 1:29 (KJV).
32. Luke 7:19-23 (KJV).
33. Mark 16:15-20 (KJV).
34. Proverbs 4:20-22 (NIV).
35. John 8:32.

Chapter Three

1. Psalm 118:22; Matthew 21:42; Mark 12:10; Luke 20:17.
2. Acts 17:28.
3. John 6:48.
4. John 10:10.
5. Isaiah 61:1.
6. John 6:48.
7. Matthew 4:4: Luke 4:4.
8. Matthew 14:17.
9. Matthew 14:20.
10. Mark 6:34 (NKJV).
11. John 6:35.
12. John 6:40.
13. Romans 8:38-39.
14. Luke 8:11-15 (NIV).
15. 2 Timothy 3:16 (NKJV).
16. Romans 8:15 (Weymouth).
17. Romans 8:17 (KJV).
18. John 15:15.
19. Ecclesiastes 4:12.
20. 1 Timothy 3:16 (NKJV).

21. Hebrews 13:5 (NKJV).
22. Psalm 139:7-10 (NKJV).
23. John 14:16.
24. John 14:17-18 (emphasis in original).
25. Deuteronomy 6:5 (NKJV).
26. Matthew 15:8 (NKJV).
27. Psalm 91:9-16 (NIV).
28. Psalm 91:14-16 (NKJV).

Chapter Four

1. Psalm 135:4 (NKJV).
2. Jeremiah 29:11 (NKJV).
3. Ephesians 2:10.
4. 2 Corinthians 5:17.
5. John 15:16 (emphasis in original).
6. 2 Corinthians 5:17.
7. Exodus 3:6.
8. Exodus 13-15.
9. John 8:58 (NKJV).
10. Hebrews 6:13.
11. Philippians 2:9.
12. Acts 4:12.
13. John. 12:28.
14. Acts 3:6.
15. Acts 3:8.
16. Acts 4:7.
17. Acts 4:17-18.
18. Philippians 2:9.
19. Revelation 2:17.
20. Romans 12:2 (AB).
21. Jeremiah 15:16.
22. Psalm 119:105.
23. Psalm 119:165.
24. 2 Corinthians 10:4-5 (NKJV).
25. Joshua 1:8.
26. Ephesians 4:20-24 (NKJV).
27. Philippians 4:8 (NKJV).

28. Daniel 6:10.
29. Joshua 1:8.
30. Psalm 29:2; Psalm 66:4; Psalm 92:1-2.

Chapter Five

1. Romans 7:18 (emphasis in original).
2. Ephesians 3:16.
3. Romans 6:1-2.
4. 1 Corinthians 9: 27.
5. Genesis 4:6-7.
6. Psalm 53:1-3; cf. Romans 3:9-12.
7. Jeremiah 23:5-6 (NKJV).
8. John 15:5-6 (NKJV).
9. Romans 11:16-18 (NKJV).
10. 2 Corinthians 5:21 (NKJV).

Chapter Six

1. Romans 8:1.
2. Galatians 5:16-17 (NKJV).
3. Matthew 18:21.
4. Matthew 18:22.
5. Matthew 18:24 (NLV).
6. Matthew 18:25 (NLV).
7. Matthew 18:25 (NLV).
8. Matthew 18:27 (NLV).
9. Matthew 18:28 (NLV).
10. Matthew 18:32-34 (NLV).
11. Matthew 18:35 (NLV).
12. Luke 23:34 (NKJV).
13. Matthew 12:31 (NKJV).
14. Matthew 5:20.
15. John 8:7.
16. Mark 11:25.
17. Mark 11:26.
18. John 15:8.
19. Proverbs 4:23.

20. Jonah 4:2 (NKJV).
21. Jonah 1:17, 2:5-6.
22. Jonah 3:1-10.
23. Jonah 4:8.
24. Jonah 4:3.
25. Jonah 4:4.
26. Psalm 94:1.
27. Jonah 3:3 and 4:11 (NKJV).
28. Jonah 4:5 (NKJV).
29. Ephesians 4:26.
30. Luke 6:28
31. Luke 6:27-28.

Chapter Seven

1. Psalm 118:8-9.
2. Psalm 146:3-4 (NKJV).
3. "Do suicides go up when the economy heads south?" Jennifer Pifer-Bixler CNN Medical Senior Producer. January 14, 2009. http://articles.cnn.com/2009-1-14/health/suicide.economy_1_lanny-berman-ponzi-scheme-rene-thierry-magon?_s=PM:HEALTH. Accessed April 12,2012.
4. 1 Timothy 6:17 (NIV).
5. Proverbs 23:18.
6. Psalm 119:114.
7. Psalm 33:20.
8. Psalm 147:11 (NIV).
9. Proverbs 13:12 (NIV).
10. Psalm 27:13 (NKJV).
11. Luke 1:37.
12. Michael Gungor and Lisa Gungor, "Dry Bones," Brash Music, 2009, MP3 Album.
13. Ezekiel 37:11 (NKJV).
14. Ezekiel 37:3 (NKJV).
15. Ezekiel 37:4-5 (NKJV).
16. Ezekiel 37:7-8 (NKJV).
17. Ezekiel 37:9-10 (NKJV).
18. Ezekiel 37:14 (NKJV).

Chapter Eight

1. Revelation 20:3 (NKJV).
2. 1 Peter 5:8.
3. John 10:10.
4. 1 Corinthians 12:28 (NKJV).
5. Philippians 4:13 (NKJV).
6. Deuteronomy 31:6.
7. Revelation 2:19 (NKJV).
8. James 2:18.
9. James 2:14-19 (NKJV).
10. Matthew 5:16 (NKJV).
11. Matthew 25:31-46.
12. Matthew 25:41.
13. Daniel 12:3 (NKJV).
14. Ephesians 6:12 (NKJV).
15. Ephesians 6:11 (NKJV).
16. Acts 10:38 (NKJV).
17. Colossians 2:15 (NKJV).
18. Colossians 2:9-10 (NKJV).
19. Proverbs 15:22 (NKJV).
20. Proverbs 11:14 (NKJV).
21. Substance Abuse and Mental Health Services Administration, *National Household Survey on Drug Abuse: Main Findings 1992* (Washington, DC: US Government Printing Office, 1994).
22. US Department of Justice, *Alcohol and Crime* (Washington, DC: US Government Printing Office, 1998).
23. "Alcohol Kills More Than AIDS, TB or Violence: WHO," Stephanie Nebehay, Reuters, accessed March 1, 2012, http://www.reuters.com/article/2011/02/11/us-alcohol-idUSTRE71A2FM20110211.
24. Hosea 4:6.
25. 1 Corinthians 6:9-10.
26. Proverbs 23:29-30 (NCV).
27. Proverbs 23:32 (NCV).
28. Proverbs 23:35 (NCV).

Chapter Nine

1. Ecclesiastes 8:14 (NCV).
2. Robert H. Schuller, *Turning Hurts Into Halos*, (Nashville: Thomas Nelson Publishers, 1999), 2.
3. Ephesians 6:12 (NKJV).
4. 2 Corinthians 12:7.
5. Galatians 4:13-15.
6. Philippians 3:14.
7. Isaiah 53:2 (KJV).
8. Romans 8:28.
9. 2 Corinthians 12:10 (NKJV).
10. Ephesians 4:27 (NIV).
11. Job 1:21.
12. Job 1:22.
13. Job 2:10.
14. Job 38:2.
15. Job 42:11.
16. Job 42:10-17.
17. James 5:11(NKJV).
18. Genesis 37:4.
19. Genesis 39:3.
20. Genesis 41:41.
21. Genesis 45:5-8.
22. Psalm 6:6-7.
23. Psalm 42:5 (MSG).
24. Psalm 116:7-8.
25. 1 Samuel 30:2 (emphasis in original).
26. 1 Samuel 30:4.
27. 1 Samuel 30:6.
28. Psalm 39:2 (emphasis in original).
29. Proverbs 15:23 (NKJV).
30. Proverbs 16:24 (NKJV).
31. 1 Kings 18:19.
32. 1 Kings 18:22-24.
33. 1 Kings 18:28.
34. 1 Kings 18:35.
35. 1 Kings 18:38-39.

36. 1 Kings 19:4.
37. 1 Kings 19:10, 14.
38. 1 Kings 19:15-16 (KJV).
39. 2 Thessalonians 1:4.

Chapter Ten

1. "What is the definition of praise?," Dictionary.com, accessed April 11, 2012 http://dictionary.reference.com/browse/praise.
2. Exodus 15:11 (KJV).
3. Exodus 15:11 (KJV).
4. 1 Chronicles 16:25.
5. Psalm 47:7.
6. Psalm 100:5 (KJV).
7. Psalm 100:4.
8. Psalm 118:24.
9. Strong, James. Strong's Exhaustive Concordance of The Bible. Maine: Hendrickson Publishers, 1990.
10. 2 Chronicles 20:1.
11. 2 Chronicles 20:3.
12. 2 Chronicles 20:15.
13. 2 Chronicles 20:18-19.
14. 2 Chronicles 20:20.
15. 2 Chronicles 20:21 (emphasis in original).
16. 2 Chronicles 20:22.
17. 2 Chronicles 20:28.
18. Acts 16:25-26 (NKJV).
19. John 10:10.
20. Isaiah 61:3 (NKJV).
21. 2 Corinthians 6:10 (NIV).
22. Acts 27:22 (NCV)
23. Habakkuk 3:17-19 (ESV).
24. Isaiah 61:3 (NKJV).
25. Psalm 69:30.
26. Job 19:25 (NKJV).
27. Isaiah 61:3 (NKJV).
28. 1 Samuel 16:14.
29. Ibid.

30. 1 Samuel 16:16.
31. 1 Samuel 16:18.
32. 1 Samuel 16:23.

Chapter Eleven

1. John 9:1-3 (NKJV).
2. Proverbs 12:25 (NKJV).
3. Ezekiel 30:15 (NKJV).
4. Ezekiel 30:16 (NKJV).
5. John 5:5 (NKJV).
6. John 5:14 (NKJV).
7. Leviticus 26:39; Ezra 9:7, 9:13; Proverbs 5:22; Isaiah 59:12, 64:7; Jeremiah 30:15.
8. Exodus 34:7, Numbers 14:18.
9. John 9:1-3.
10. Acts 10:38.
11. Job 2:7.
12. Matthew 9:32, Matthew 12:22, Luke 9:42.
13. Luke 13:11 (NKJV).
14. Luke 10:26-28.
15. Luke 10:30-37.
16. James 5:13-14.
17. 1 Thessalonians 5:17.
18. 2 Timothy 1:3.
19. Romans 12:12 (NKJV).
20. Colossians 4:12.
21. John 17:20 (NKJV).
22. Acts 12:5 (NKJV).
23. Acts 12:7 (NKJV).
24. Acts 12:10 (NKJV).
25. Acts 12:11 (NKJV).
26. James 5:16.
27. Romans 2:29.
28. Matthew 23:27
29. Romans 5:6.
30. Isaiah 61:1.
31. Matthew 18:14 (KJV).

32. James 3:9.
33. Genesis 1:31.
34. John 13:34
35. 1 John 4:12.
36. John 13:35.
37. Matthew 22:36-40 (KJV).
38. James 3:8-12 (KJV).